Churchyard Epiphany

Leila White

Clink
Street

London | New York

Published by Clink Street Publishing 2020

First edition.

This book is for information only, and is not intended as a replacement for medical treatment or advice.

ISBN:
paperback: 978-1-913962-68-5
ebook: 978-1-913962-69-2

With love to my family
Norman,
Donald, Colin, Jamie
and grandchildren
Ella
Liam & Cameron
Monty & Rufus

And to my friends in the church

Who are we to say that today's antibiotics and high-tech medicine will always be available? In a world of increasing violence, war and disaster, a breakdown in the nation's health service might happen at any time, thus curtailing production of insulin for the diabetic, steroids for the hormone-deficient, and anti-coagulants for the thrombotic. High-technology can do little without its specialised equipment. There may come a time when we shall have to rely on our own natural resources. It would be then that a knowledge of alternatives could be vital to survival.

– Thomas Bartram, Fellow of
the National Institute of Medical Herbalists 1995

Preface

From my earliest years I have always appreciated plants, and I knew most of the wild flowers growing near my home. During the 1950s Brooke Bond Tea launched two collections of Wild Flower cards, it gave great pleasure to stick the latest pictures into the developing books.

The I-Spy books were around then too, both were enormously useful for the curious child.

On a visit to my Shetland Grandmother, Loma, my aunt introduced me to the flowers growing there. I learned how to press them between sheets of blotting paper, and slip them under the rug to help the process along. This was at a time when schools encouraged nature studies, and indeed this helped me gain the top prize, the Ladybird Book of British Wild Flowers. It was the only school prize I was ever to get, Being a member of the Girl Guides also gave me a chance to learn more.

Entry into the world of grown ups pushed plants firmly into the back ground.

This interest was to be rekindled many years later at the school gate. I discovered new friends who were practicing alternative therapies, or studying herbalism, At that time I found out about my herbalist great grandmother and great great grandmother's dependancy on plants as a means of healing. The turning point was a trip with my friend Pam to the Wisley Gardens in Surrey. The gardens were fabulous, but more importantly I bought a book which would change my life. 'The Apothecary's Garden' by Anne McIntyre.

Medicinal plants from Achillea to Viola were featured. More importantly it gave an informative herb and ailment chart. This encouraged me to create my own herb garden, plants that were then turned into tinctures, teas and ointments for my own use. I then studied herb related therapies for a few years.

In 2009 I started work on the Herbcraft Academy Course, it was then I started noticing the churchyard plants. Initially a few were discovered, which I wrote about for the local magazine. I thought I might find ten, but the number surpassed fifty, then one hundred, it was the churchyard that kept on giving.

The tiny speedwell, Veronica verna was the very last, but who knows ?

Plant List

The plants are organised using the up-to-date family groupings featured in Simon Harrap's Wild Flowers.

Alliaceae

Daffodil   *Narcissus pseudonarcissus*
Snowdrop   *Galanthus nivalis*

Amaranthaceae

Good Hing Henry   *Chenopodium bonus-henricus*

Apiaceae or Umbellifers

Cow parsley   *Anthriscus sylvestris*
Common Hogweed   *Heracleum sphondylium*
Ground Elder   *Aegopodium podagraria*

Araceae

Cuckoo Pint   *Arum maculatum*

Araliaceae

Ivy   *Hedera helix*

Asparagaceae

Star of Bethlehem   *Ornithogalum umbellatum*
Bluebell   *Hyacinthoides non-scriptus*
Spring Squill   *Scilla verna*

Asteraceae Compositae

Ragwort	*Senecio jacobaea*
Groundsel	*Senecio vulgaris*
Coltsfoot	*Tussilago farfara*
Daisy	*Bellis perennis*
Mayweed	*Matricaria cotula*
Pineapple Mayweed	*Matricaria discoidea*
Yarrow	*Achillea millefolium*
Ox-eyed daisy	*Leucanthemum vulgare*
Burdock	*Arctium Lappa*
Knapweed	*Centaurea nigra*
Mugwort	*Artemisia vulgaris*
Dandelion	*Taraxacum officinale*
Cat's ear	*Hypochaeris radicata*
Goat's beard	*Tragopogon pratensis*
Bristly ox tongue	*Helminthotheca echioides*
Perennial Sow-Thistle	*Sonchus arvensis*
Smooth Sow Thistle	*Sonchus oleraceus*
Hawkweeds	*Hieracium aug.*
Hawkbits	*Leontodon hispidus*
Hawksbeard smooth	*Crepis capillaris*
Spear thistle	*Cirsium vulgare*
Creeping thistle	*Cirsium arvense*
Woolly thistle	*Cirsium eriophorum*
Slender thistle	*Carduus tenuiflorus*

Boraginaceae

Forget-me-not	*Myosotis arvensis*

Brassicaceae – Cabbage Family

Charlock	*Sinapis arvensis*
Shepherd's Purse	*Capsella bursa-pastoris*
Common whitlow grass	*Erophila verna*

Cuckoo flower	*Cardamine pratensis*
Garlic Mustard	*Alliaria petiolata*

Caprifoliaceae

Elder	*Sambucus nigra*
Honeysuckle	*Lonicera periclymenum*

Caryophyllaceae

Red campion	*Silene dioica*
White campion	*Silene latifolia*
Greater stitchwort	*Stellaria holostea*
Chickweed	*Stellaria media*

Clusiaceae

St John's wort	*Hypericum perforatum*

Convolvulaceae

Field bindweed	*Convolvulus arvensis*
Hedge bindweed	*Calystegia sepium*

Crassulaceae

Orpine	*Sedum telephium*

Cucurbitaceae

White bryony	*Bryonia dioica*

Dioscoreaceae

Black bryony	*Tamus communis*

Dipsacaceae

Scabious field	*Knautia arvensis*

Equisetaceae

Horsetail   *Equestum arvense*

Euphorbia

Dog's mercury   *Mercurialis perennis*

Fabaceae – Clovers

Red clover   *Trifolium pratense*
White clover   *Trifolium repens*
Black medick   *Medicago lupulina*
Birdsfoot trefoil   *Lotus corniculatus*
Tufted vetch   *Vicia cracca*
Meadow vetchling   *Lathyrus pratensis*

Geraniaceae

Herb Robert   *Geranium robertianum*
Meadow crane's bill   *Geranium pratense*
Dove's foot   *Geranium molle*

Gramineae – Grasses

Couch grass   *Agropyron repens*
Oat   *Avena sativa*
Barley   *Hordeum distichon*

Iridaceae

Gladwyn   *Iris foetidissima*

Lamiaceae Dead nettles and mints

Wild marjoram   *Origanum vulgare*
Wild basil   *Clinopodium vulgare*
Self heal   *Prunella vulgaris*

Black horehound	*Ballota nigra*
Hedge Woundwort	*Stachys sylvatica*
Archangel	*Lamium album*
Red dead nettle	*Lamium purpureum*
Henbit	*Lamium amplexicaule*
Ground ivy	*Glechoma hederacae*
Bugle	*Ajuga reptans*

Malvaceae – Mallows

Common mallow	*Malva sylvestris*
Musk mallow	*Malva moschata*

Onagraceae

Rose-bay willow-herb	*Chamerion angustifolium*
Willow-herb	*Epilobium spp.*

Plantaginaceae – Plantains

Greater plantain	*Plantago major*
Ribwort plantain	*Plantago lanceolata*
Hoary plantain	*Plantago media*
Foxglove	*Digitalis purpurea*
Germander speedwell	*Veronica chamaedrys*
Spring Speedwell	*Veronica verna*

Polygonaceae

Bistort	*Persicaria bistorta*
Redshank	*Persicaria maculosa*
Common sorrel	*Rumex acetosa*
Sheep's sorrel	*Rumex acetosella*
Broad leaf dock	*Rumex obtusifolius*
Yellow dock	*Rumex crispus*
Clustered Dock	*Rumex conglomeratus*

Primulaceae

Primrose	*Primula vulgaris*
Cowslip	*Primula veris*
Creeping Jenny	*Lysimachia nummularia*
Scarlet pimpernel	*Anagallis arvensis*

Ranunculaceae

Buttercup Ranunculus	*Ranunculus bulbosus*
Meadow buttercup	*Ranunculus acris*
Creeping buttercup	*Ranunculus repens*
Goldilocks buttercup	*Ranunculus auricomus*
Wood anemone	*Anemone nemorosa*
Lesser celandine	*Ficaria verna*

Rosaceae

Dog rose	*Rosa canina*
Blackberry	*Rubus fruticosus*
Blackthorn	*Prunus spinosa*
Bullace	*Prunus domestica*
Wood aven	*Geum urbanium*
Barren strawberry	*Potentilla sterilise*
Silverweed	*Potentilla anserina*
Tormentil	*Potentilla erecta*
Cinquefoil	*Potentilla reptans*
Agrimony	*Agrimonia eupatoria*
Meadowsweet	*Spiraeae latifola Filipendula ulmaria*
Hawthorn	*Cratagus oxycantha*

Rubiaceae

Lady's bedstraw	*Galium verum*
Hedge bedstraw	*Galium album*
Upright bedstraw	*Galium subsp*
Cleavers	*Galium aparine*

Woodruff	*Galium odoratum*
Field madder	*Sherardia arvensis*

Scrophulariaceae

Dark mullein	*Verbascum nigra*

Solanaceae

Bittersweet	*Solanum dulcamara*
Black nightshade	*Solanum nigrum*

Urticaceae

Nettle	*Urtica dioica*
Nettle small	*Utrica urens*
Pellitory of the Wall	*Parietaria judaica*

Violaceae

Violet Dog	*Viola riviniana*

Mosses, lichen, ferns and fungi

Mosses	*Sphagnum cymbifolium, papillose, palustre*
Lichen	*Caloplaca flavenscens*
Hart's tongue fern	*Phyllitis scolopendrium*
Wall rue	*Asplenium Ruta-muraria*
Lady fern	*Athyrium filix-femina*
Psilocybin	*Psilocybe semilanceata*
Puffball	*Lycoperdon perlatum*

The plants are set out in their family groups. I found a few changes to where the plants are now placed. In recent years there are some new family groupings, foxglove and speedwell are now in the Plantaginaceae family.

Trees

The trees families are as set out in Tony Russell's What's That Tree?

Aceraceae

Field maple	*Acer campestre*
Sycamore	*Acer pseudoplatanus*

Aquifoliaceae

Holly	*Ilex aquifolium*

Betulaceae

Hazel	*Corylus avellana*

Fagaceae

Oak	*Quercus roubo*
Holm oak	*Quercus ilex ballota*

Oleaceae

Ash	*Fraxinus excelsior*
Lilac	*Syringa vulgaris*

Pinaceae

Atlantic cedar	*Cedrus atlantica*

Taxaceae

Yew   *Taxus baccata*

Tiliaceae

Lime   *Tilia x europaea*

Ulmaceae

Elm   *Ulmus procera*
Wych elm   *Ulmus glabra*

Opening Chapter

Like plants, this book grew organically. I did not sit, pencil poised at page one to work through chapter by chapter, rather it developed. This process was often dictated by what I found from one season to the next. Nothing was, or could have been planned in advance.

In the mid nineties I gave up teaching to learn about plant based therapies, an Herbal course, followed by Aromatherapy then Bach Flower Remedies. I studied Complementary and Alternative Therapies used in cancer care, and indeed I gained the first module of a Master's Degree offered by Exeter University and Bristol Cancer Help Centre. A long period of illness followed, which put studies on hold. Many years later I met herbalist Melanie Cardwell when she was introducing her herbal studies course, Herbcraft Academy.

I launched myself into the course, and it was at that period that I found myself in a small country churchyard, noticing the very many plants that were growing there. This led to writing short articles on the finds in two local magazines. As the writing built up, the next stage seemed to be a book. Many of the chapters were written some time ago. The whole process has been stop start, as many momentous things were happening in my life. As I write this, the end is only days away… the whole should be in the post to the publisher very soon !

Recently a friend presented me with a yellowed newspaper cutting that she had found in a second hand book. "I thought this would interest you" she said, indeed it did!

It was an article by Alison Ross (AR) entitled 'Wildlife Sanctuary in a Village Churchyard'. The exact date or the newspaper is a mystery, but there is a clue, there are quotes from Sir Edward Salisbury who died in 1978, and they are recorded in the present tense. Sir Edward Salisbury, botanist, was the director of the Royal Botanic Gardens, Kew from 1943 to 1956. He was responsible for the restoration of the gardens after the Second World War. "Sir Edward as a botanist bemoans the destruction of so many interesting wild or long naturalised plants."

The material in the article is fascinating. AR records the days some twelve years previously when 'Old Bert' used to maintain the churchyard by scything down the grasses three or four times a year. Bert prepared himself by pulling on his tallest boots and making sure his trouser legs were securely tied to prevent any snakes taking refuge from the scythe in his clothing.

All manner of creatures great and small inhabited the safety of the churchyard; insects, butterflies, beetles and spiders too.

"Medicinally useful plants also grew frequently in churchyards and Sir Edward suggests that the herb-women deliberately planted out many of their remedies on 'holy land', knowing that they would be safe as well as insuring their accessibility." AR

The desire for tidy churchyards probably started some fifty years ago, and visitors to the graves prefer it so. Therefore

I regard myself as exceedingly fortunate to have been in the right churchyard at the right time. Throughout the churchyard there are many medicinal plants, the trees, hedgerows, wildflowers, mushrooms and lichens. I have a tally of more than 130 plants that have been used for medicinal purposes at some point in time. My favourite place was the old graves, a veritable tangle of pink, yellow, white and mauve flowers. I use an iPhone to take pictures of the plants, and often discovering more when inspecting the images at home on my computer; finding another of great interest in the background, what a bonus!

Today the graveyard is beautifully neat and tidy, hardly a blade of grass out of place. Many kerb stones on the old graves have been removed so that a large mowing machine can move with ease over them. Nature conservation was considered, and an area has been set aside to allow the wildflowers to flourish. They do of course, but only a limited few, namely the black knapweed, bird's foot trefoil, meadow vetchling, and purple vetch, which have availed themselves of this at present. It has been observed that the growing conditions vary from the area of the old graves to the lower ground by the hedge to the east, therefore attracting different species of plant.

The wild area to the north of the church, thistles, nettles, burdock, ragwort, sow thistles and dog's mercury thrived; that area too has been cleared. The area hugging the flint walls has been trimmed back. The parishioners are happy, it all looks so good. After all it is a graveyard. It is a very pleasing and well maintained 'God's Acre'.

In his book *Earth to Earth: A Natural History of Churchyards*, Stefan Buczacki describes how the make up of the churchyard materials promote the growth of the flowers. He tells of how the rocks beneath the ground dictate whether the soil will be alkaline or acid. This determines the plants likely to grow in it. Firstly, aeons ago the mosses formed, and they through time broke down, thus enriching the loam and making an attractive base for future plants. Today gardeners appreciate the value of the moss to improve the plants in their own plots. Unfortunately the desire to achieve the best results for the gardener is damaging the landscape in the wilder parts of Britain as gardens make much of this natural commodity.

Within a churchyard with the right base, the flowers will flourish. Seemingly there are about 6,000 churchyards now left undisturbed for this purpose. Many graveyards became over populated in Victorian times, and whilst the church continues to be used for services the graveyards are left to naturalise.

Thus many churchyards were closed for new burials and while the church itself may have continued in regular use, the burial ground often became neglected. It began to return to the surrounding landscape from which it was born and only in recent times has it been properly appreciated how valuable these ancient havens are for conserving and enhancing their flora and fauna; what, over the past thirty years, has been called their biodiversity. – Stefan Buczacki

I take heart though, after reading *The Running Hare*. This joyous book is written by farmer John Lewis-Stempel, (JLS). As the book title suggests he longed for the return of the hares, and after dreaming of his childhood days when he enjoyed nature as it once was, flocks of birds in the trees, butterflies, bees and… hares, he set about finding a piece of land he could rent to see if it was possible to farm it using the old methods.

He found what he was looking for, a four-acre plot known as Flinders Field, in South Herefordshire. It included a few acres of woodland too. In effect his book is a diary of how he progressed the renting of the field with the purpose of encouraging birds back; growing wildflowers amongst the wheat, and most importantly creating a habitat for the hare. It is by turn whimsical and exceedingly informative.

John Lewis-Stempel shares with his readers his knowledge of farming methods of times gone by. The reality is that even one hundred years ago farming continued along the lines of our forefathers throughout the centuries. The greatest problem as he sees it is the use of chemicals. He describes a moment when he gained access to his neighbour's field to investigate the soil, hard and compacted without a single worm. He quotes Charles Darwin stating that arable land contains up to 53,000 worms per acre. "Not in this field, not in this time," he observes.

He succeeded in cultivating by using the old methods, and when planting the corn broadcast the seeds. He added corn marigold, corn chamomile, cornflower and corn poppy around the edges for good measure.

By the end of the farming year JLS had achieved his goals. His patch was a delight of flora and fauna. More particularly he produced a haven for the hares.

He also observed that not only had the flower seeds flourished, but a good number of wild flowers had arrived by themselves. The following list only includes those that are grown in my churchyard:

Scarlet pimpernel
Speedwell
Forget-me-not

Thistle
Hedge bindweed
Shepherd's purse
Groundsel
Docks
Wild Oats
Docks
Nettles

Many seeds lie dormant for years, and given a chance, these plants will eventually flourish again.

JLS mentions churchyards and the part played by the incumbents. Vicars in the past spent a great deal of time in God's Acre and made observations on the natural world from their view point. Perhaps the most famous writer was Rev. Gilbert White of Selbourne, Hampshire. As a naturalist he commented on birds, animals, trees and flowers; and of great significance he recorded the volcanic eruption on Iceland known as Laki. It started on 8th June 1783 and continued for eight months. The smokey fog effectively blocked the sun so vital for the survival of crops, therefore ruining harvests. It is thought that 10,000 people died as a result, mainly of famine.

On a visit to St Michael's Church in Dulas Herefordshire, JLS writes:

> It is like looking back in time, to the age before agricultural 'improvement'. The wild daffodils are now over, but the bluebells are coming out to join the primroses, the cowslips, the violets. Later there will be greater butterfly orchids, betony, black knapweed, tormentil, yellow rattle and quaking grass – and all beasts and bugs who love and live on them. – JLS

With the exception of three plants, that could be my churchyard.

Like a vicar, as organist of my small church, I too spend time very regularly and often, observing the passing seasons, and the many passing plants.

Hares.

How I longed to see hares too. In 1986 our family moved into the countryside. We were surrounded by farm fields, but never a hare to be seen. Deer, snakes, squirrels, migrating geese, etc., but never a hare. Some twenty years later we moved further north, again surrounded by farm fields, and also ancient woodlands. Occasionally hares were spotted, but never close. One summer's evening I was leaning on a farm gate watching the sun set behind the church when I spotted a young hare approaching. I stood stalk still, hardly daring to breathe, lest I startled it. He ran under the gate only inches from me. Wow.

Our home was within a small community close to the church where the plants were found. One day my husband drew my attention to a rather wet leveret, huddled behind a plant pot for safe keeping. Previously we had glimpsed mum running between the houses. Had she perhaps put her baby there to stay put until she could collect him? His coat was quite reddish in colour.

With regards churchyards, I have a treasured a memory of my own. On a visit to another churchyard in a nearby village, I discovered the old graves, obstructed by trees. The one that really touched me was a stone bearing the name

Violet, the grave of a girl of twelve years. I saw it in the spring, and the whole grave was covered in Violets.

*Wildlife Sanctuary in a Village
Churchyard*   Alison Ross
The Running Hare   John-Lewis Stempel
Earth to Earth   Stefan Buczacki
The Natural History of Selbourne   Rev. Gilbert White

Part One

Alliaceae

Daffodil *Narcissus pseudonarcissus*

> "For oft, when on my couch I lie
> In vacant or in pensive mood,
> They flash upon that inward eye
> Which is the bliss of solitude;
> And then my heart with pleasure fills,
> And dances with the daffodils."
>
> – William Wordsworth

After the bleakness of winter our spirits can be lifted by seeing bright yellow daffodils; they are all around us, in the home and in the garden. They bring a great feeling of hope that spring is on the way. Often known as the lent lily, they are closely connected to Mothering Sunday, Easter, and St David's Day.

Culpeper used the daffodil as an emetic and purgative, in small quantities only. For external use it could be used to alleviate aching joints. Today the daffodil has found favour as a possible treatment for Alzheimer's disease.

Snowdrop *Galanthus nivalis*

Also known as the fair maid of February, candle-mass bells, Mary's tapers.

According to legend, an Angel appeared to Adam and Eve after their expulsion from the Garden of Eden and offered the snowdrop as a sign of hope; for us it brings the thought of the approaching spring. On a visit to the churchyard in February one is met with huge swathes of this welcoming plant.

Not a native British plant, the snowdrop originated in the cold regions of the Caucuses. A few were recorded in English gardens during the 16th century, however during the Crimean War the soldiers were attracted to this pretty little plant, flowering white among the carnage of the battlefields. Bulbs were brought home to Britain, where they now flourish.

It is more than just a pretty flower! It has been used to treat neuritis and neuralgia, myasthenia gravis (chronic muscle weakness), myopathy as well as post-polio paralysis. Today there are studies going on to see if the galantamine properties within the plant can alleviate the symptoms of Alzheimer's disease.

Have we always known about the properties of the snowdrop? Many of us remember the story of Odysseus and his encounter with the Goddess Circe. She bewitched his sailors by muddling their brains and turning them into swine. Hermes intervened, and gave Odysseus 'Moly' to restore the wits to his sailors. In 1983 two scholars suggested that 'Moly' was in fact, the snowdrop.

It is certainly a plant of hope!

Amaranthaceae Goosefoots

Good King Henry *Chenopodium bonus-henricus*

Found growing on the poorest land this plant was a useful food, and quite similar to spinach. It was also used as a diuretic and a treatment for scurvy.

Apiaceae or Umbellifers

Cow parsley *Anthriscus sylvestris*

This plant is often known as Queen Anne's Lace. When seen around the edge of a crop field, one can see how it got its common name. The name may have come from Queen Anne, wife of James I, who was said to have been an excellent lace-maker, or Queen Anne who ruled Great Britain in until her death in 1714.

As this plant is becoming more abundant there are concerns that it is causing the demise of other wildflowers. The use of fertilisers in the fields, and the practice of leaving the grass cuttings on the verges causes enrichment to the soil. Most wildflowers choose poor soil.

In many parts of the country it was thought unlucky to bring cow parsley into the house, and it was given names like 'dead man's flourish' or 'kill your mother quick'. This did not refer to any poisons, but more to superstitions. It is not the only plant that is unwelcome in the home as a harbinger of doom, many flowers are regarded as 'unlucky'.

There are a number of claims made for this plant, for treating respiratory problems, anti-stress, insomnia, diabetes, and recent research indicates that cow parsley has the potential to help treat Alzheimer's, Crohn's and Parkinson's diseases.

For horses suffering from laminitis, a hot infusion of cow parsley can bring about relief to the suffering animals.

Cow parsley flourishes on the west side of the church, in the fairly open grass areas.

Common Hogweed *Heracleum sphondylium*

As the Latin name suggests, the plant was named after the god Hercules, renowned for his great strength. The English name reflects the plants use as fodder for pigs and cattle.

In the past the seeds of hogweed were boiled in oil, and applied to rashes, shingles and running sores. Culpeper used a preparation of the seeds to treat running ears.

Today hogweed is being used as an alternative treatment for both male and female infertility. The use of hogweed for sexual problems seems to be common practice in Eastern Europe, and it is known as 'Romanian ginseng'. It is claimed to stimulate the ovaries and improve the quality of sperm. It is sold as a tincture, as tea bags and even for homeopathic preparations. Seemingly, quite a wonder drug, and promoted for infertility.

In by-gone days boys often used the dried stalk as a pea shooter.

WARNING. Hogweed must not be confused with the giant hogweed. Heracleum mantegazzianum a highly dangerous plant, and not found in the churchyard, but it is found a mile away. It has statuesque proportions, giant exotic and decorative leaves and a large imposing flower head. This striking plant was beloved of Victorian gardeners, and over a period of time has escaped from the flower beds. It now can be found growing along footpaths and river banks. On contact with the sap it can prove very damaging to the skin The sap is not painful, but when exposed to the sunlight the toxins are activated causing damage to the skin, which is known as phytophotodermatitis. The results of damage might not appear for a day or two. Should you be unfortunate enough to encounter this plant and make contact with the sap, treat it immediately. It needs to be removed with a tissue, taking great care not to rub the skin. The skin must be washed thoroughly, and be kept out of the sunlight for a couple of days. In severe cases scarring can last for years.

Ground Elder *Aegopodium podagraria*

Also known as gout weed, bishop's weed, herb gerard.

This plant is extremely unpopular with gardeners. It is almost impossible to get rid of. The 17th century herbalist Gerard said of it: "So fruitful in his increase that where it hath once taken roote, it will hardly be gotten out again, spoiling and getting every year more ground, to the annoying of better herbes."

How such a menacing plant was brought to this country is debatable, some claim that it was the Romans, others say with the Normans at the times of conquest. Ground elder later found its way (very probably invited) into the monastery gardens, and was used by the monks to treat gout with seemingly great effect.

In Culpeper's day it was known as goutweed, and that is just what it was used to relieve; this is confirmed by the scientific name, the Greek aigos for goat; podos for foot, and the Latin podagra meaning gout.

It was also valued in the treatment of the other painful conditions of sciatica, aching joints and cold pains. Even today it can help alleviate these ailments

Poultices can be made by boiling the roots and leaves, and applying to the affected parts. The Swedish botanist

Linnaeus considered it a good spring vegetable! The leaves of ground elder are eaten, it is said, in Russia and Lithuania.

Ground elder is not related to the elder tree.

Araceae

Cuckoo Pint *Arum maculatum*

Common names are lords and ladies, snake's head, Adam and Eve, naked boys, Jack in the pulpit, cows and bulls, and many, many more!

Cuckoo pint is a small plant, and found in shady places; an extraordinary plant, having an exotic look to it. The name has nothing to do with cuckoos, but more describes the rather risqué and suggestive nature of the shape of the plant, one seemingly that Queen Victoria disapproved of !

In the early summer the green hood (known as the spathe) opens to reveal the brown spandix. Contained at the base of the hood are the male and female flowers, and above the flowers are a ring of hairs to trap the flies that will pollenate the plant. In late summer all that is left of the plant is a stalk of brightly coloured red, orange and yellow berries.

It is a very poisonous plant in its fresh form. It ceases to be poisonous when dried. In the olden days the dried tuber was used for food. On the Isle of Portland, cuckoo pint was harvested and became known as Portland arrowroot. This made a gruel that was given to nourish sick people.

Cuckoo pint does have some medicinal qualities, and the root was once used as an ointment to relieve the pain of gout and rheumatism. It was said to alleviate the symptoms of sore throats. Today it is only used by homeopaths.

A more practical alternative name is 'root starch'. In times gone by the root starch was used by the Elizabethans to stiffen their hair and beards. It was used also for starching clothes and ruffs, although it was observed by Gerard that the hands of the laundress were "choppeth, blistereth, and maketh hands rough and rugged and withall smarting."

This starch was made into a cosmetic paste to whiten the skin. This was used by Queen Elizabeth I; white faces were the fashion statements of the day!

Araliaceae

Ivy *Hedera helix*

Ivy has long been used as a treatment for coughs, chest and bronchial congestion. It works as an expectorant, which means that it can help to loosen mucus from the respiratory tract; thus making it easier to expel the mucus from the lungs.

Ivy also has anti-spasmodic properties which will help with coughing fits. The product Ivy-Thyme Complex is a tincture (made by extracting the properties of the plant in alcohol) and this is taken a few drops at a time in water. It is said to do much to alleviate the aforementioned conditions. The tincture would be more suitable for diabetics than the usual cough mixtures which often contain a great deal of sugar.

A very useful plant of great value to florists, and the leaves have been used as templates for the carvings around the church.

Asparagaceae

Star of Bethlehem *Ornithogalum umbellatum*

On my frequent visits to the churchyard I usually knew what I might find as one season moves into the next. One sunny summer evening in May I had a surprise find. In the area of the old graves in amongst the long grass I spotted some white flowers. They were really well hidden in the grass, it was fortunate they caught my eye. The flowers had closed for the night, but I noticed the green stripe on the back of the petals, it was Star of Bethlehem, and it was the first time I had ever seen it.

This small shining white plant has perfect six-fold geometry, and this arrangement has been used in antiquity to suggest the matter of Divinity; one triangle representing the Divine touching the earth, the other the material world extending upwards to God.

In medicine, the Star of Bethlehem was once used to treat congestive heart failure. It contains two digitalis like glycosides, digitalis is also present in the foxglove. Both are used for heart conditions, and both highly dangerous if used without medical advice.

Homeopaths prepare a tincture using the bulbs of Star of Bethlehem to treat some types of cancer. It is also used in Bach Flower Remedies.

Bluebell *Hyacinthoides non-scriptus*

English bluebells are a sight to gladden hearts. Alfred Lord Tennyson describes them as "the heaven's up-breaking through the earth," and given the vast carpets that they form in the woods, it certainly looks like it! To accompany this feast for the eyes, the bluebell has the most delicate and delicious fragrance. In the olden days it was used medicinally, as a diuretic, styptic, and as a cure for snake bites. None of these treatments would be recognised today as the bluebell is now regarded as a poisonous plant.

Once upon a time the bluebell was use as a gluey substance, to stiffen lace ruffs and to firm the binding of books. The fletcher used the bluebell to affix the feathers to his arrows.

Bluebells are becoming rare; it is a criminal offence to gather the bulbs as they are a protected species.

Spring squill *Scilla verna*

This plant is spreading itself between the hedge to the south of the churchyard and the first grave. It certainly looks as if it has been planted there, perhaps because of the name Cilla? Who knows. It is other members of this plant family that have the medicinal properties. Very lovely to behold.

Asteraceae Compositae

All of these plants have a daisy-like appearance.

Ragwort *Senecio jacobaea*

Once upon a time when Culpeper was an herbalist, the juice of ragwort was found useful for cleaning and healing 'old filthy ulcers', and internal ulcers. It was helpful in cases of sciatica, aches and pains.

Today there is absolutely nothing redeeming about the ragwort. Living in the countryside, everyone who owns or loves horses will root out every last piece of the plant. It did grow at the north side of the church, but now all the anti-social plants have been removed.

Plants do come and go. At the moment it is truly out of fashion. This is a powerful plant, perhaps one day scientists might find a really useful treatment from the chemical compounds within the plant to save us from some future condition.

Groundsel *Senecio vulgaris*

Dioscorides used groundsel with wine to make a medicine to relieve pains in the stomach that resulted from too much bile. He also recommended it for jaundice, and epilepsy. Kidney stones might be expelled by taking groundsel.

It grows in rough ground, and is found to the north of the church. It is the whole plant that is used, collected in May, and dried for later use.

Coltsfoot *Tussilago farfara*

I have observed and studied plants since childhood, but there has been one that has eluded me, the coltsfoot. I had been told that it was like a dandelion, but with a tidier head. That is indeed true. It seemed to appear everywhere, so how had I never found it?

I knew that it was one of the earliest flowering plants in the year, I didn't appreciate just how early. The weather then is not always conducive to plant hunting, frost, snow or heavy rain probably put me off.

A few years ago I happened to be in the churchyard in May, not looking for anything in particular when I spotted what looked like a coltsfoot leaf among the old graves. It is about the size and shape of a colt's foot, but that in itself was not enough to go on. Butterbur has a very similar leaf. Coltsfoot is an interesting plant, the flower appears first, giving it the common name of 'son before the father'. The stalk is scaly, and after flowering it has the white parachute type seed heads.

The following February I was out checking the area that I had mentally marked, and started looking aided by Freda, Liz, Jamie, Lucy and Emily. Sure enough, we did find two heads supported by thick, purplish, scaly stems, thereafter a few more, but not many in total.

Coltsfoot has been known for centuries as a treatment for winter ailments. The Latin name for cough and cold is 'tussis', therefore the Latin name 'Tussilago farfara'. From the time of the earliest written records, Coltsfoot had been the remedy for coughs, colds, bronchitis, mild asthma and even whooping cough.

Treatment was simply making an infusion of some flower-heads, or the leaves.

Lozenges were made from the coltsfoot and brown sugar, and kept for use in the winter. This led to the manufacture of coltsfoot rock by confectioners Stockley's Sweets, of Oswaldtwistle in Lancashire.

Coltsfoot has a few other uses, the crushed leaves can be a comfort to ulcers, swellings and bites.

The silky seed head, the pappus, were collected by children in the Highlands to stuff pillows. Goldfinches collect this too for their nests.

The leaves are saved as tinder, either as they are, or treated with saltpetre as a fire lighter.

Coltsfoot leaves give a greenish-yellow dye.

All in all, a very versatile plant, and fine if it is happily growing in the countryside, and not in the garden. The underground stems survive for long periods, and often appear after the ground has been disturbed. For all its virtues, it is exceedingly difficult to get rid of.

Daisy *Bellis perennis*

Also known as the day's eye, bruisewort

> Daisies are our silver
> Buttercups our gold:
> This is all the treasure
> We can have or hold
> — Jan Struther

The daisy really needs no introduction, and for many older folks it might have been the first plant that was recognised. It can bring back memories of long summer days, perhaps the happy hours spent making of daisy chains; or using the daisy as an oracle to ascertain their love interests while picking off one petal after another until they were left with the answer. The question of "He loves me, he loves me not" could raise or dash the hopes of the love lorn.

The daisy can be used as a treatment for bruising, as the old name suggests. The crushed leaves can be applied to wounds to help healing, Herbalists might make a tincture to purify the blood, thus helping treat skin diseases and boils. Also it can be used for coughs and catarrh; arthritis and rheumatism.

In homeopathy the daisy is used for the treatment of sprains, bruises, spots and eczema.

It is said that summer has arrived when one can put a foot on seven daisies. Generally, that might apply to the whole year round now-a-days as a result of global warming.

Mayweed *Anthemis cotula*

According to Culpeper, mayweed has some of the virtues of chamomile, but has a far more disagreeable taste.

This little plant grows at the edge of the gravel path, it seems to flower most of the year.

In the days of the old herbalists it was used to expel wind and to ease pains and aches and the joints and other parts

In the hands of an herbalist today the flowers would be used to make poultices to apply to piles. They might also make an infusion to stimulate menstruation

Pineapple Mayweed *Matricaria discoidea*

"The spread of the fruitily perfumed Pineapple Weed, which arrived in Britain from Oregon in 1871, exactly tracked the adoption of the treaded motor tyre, to which its ribbed seeds clung as if they were the soles of small climbing boots." – Richard Mabey.

Pineapple mayweed can also be found in North East Asia. The arrival date of 1871 to Britain seems to be very exact.

It is thought that this plant had some novelty value, resembling the chamomile, but without the white petals. The scent might have appealed to some. It was noted that Meriwether Lewis picked pineapple weed when on the famous Lewis and Clark expedition, by the Clearwater River in the USA. He kept it pressed in a book. Perhaps it was a curiosity, or he might have appreciated the perfume/odour of the plant, which could be either used as a perfume, or insect repellent. Might it have been kept as a memory of a romantic encounter? On their travels Lewis and Clark received the hospitality of the Native American women.

It is known that the indigenous people had a variety of uses for this plant. Women suffering menstrual cramps and anaemia found it helpful. Infections and stomach problems were also alleviated by the pineapple mayweed.

Pineapple mayweed was quite at home in the middle of the old graves in the churchyard.

Yarrow *Achillea millefolium*

Also known as soldier's woundwort, nose bleed, carpenter's weed, bloodwort, staunchweed. milfoil, old man's pepper

Yarrow's many common names suggest the external uses to which the plant might be put. 'Soldier's woundwort' was sought out and used on the battlefield, packed into wounds to staunch bleeding. The yarrow has antiseptic, astringent and wound healing qualities. The link to Achilles tells of certain stories in which Achilles knew how to use this plant to heal battle wounds.

As the 'carpenter's herb', is was a helpful first aid for the nicks and cuts caused by woodworking. And as for 'nose bleed' the name speaks for itself. A few leaves rolled into a plug and inserted into the nostril is said to be effective.

This herb is common in the countryside, and quite pretty in shades of white and pale pink. It is described as a good companion plant, as it improves the health of other plants growing around it. The flat topped multi-flower heads attract bees and pollinating insects.

Herbalists use yarrow for colds, fevers, kidney disorders, toothaches, skin irritation, stomach ulcers and abscesses. Sometimes known as a 'woman's herb' it is reputed to relieve abdominal cramps, to regulate the menses, and amenorrhea.

There is evidence to suggest yarrow has been used for at least 60,000 years. A particular grave, known as Shanidar IV, Northern Iraq, and known as the 'flower burial' was found to contain pollen of seven different plants, yarrow being one of them. All seven plants are still recognised by herbalists today as medicinal plants.

Ox-eyed daisy *Leucanthemum vulgare*

Also known as Marguerite or gowan in Scotland.

This daisy is not to be confused with the little bellis daisy. The ox-eyed is a member of the chrysanthemum family.

In Culpepper's time it was used to treat wounds internally and externally. It was said to refresh the liver and other inward parts. Culpepper claims that it could "Cureth all ulcers and postulate in the mouth or tongue, and in the secret parts"!

Herbalists today might use it in the treatment of whooping cough and asthma.

This familiar plant along with two other types of daisies where hybridised to create the Shasta daisy, a very acceptable garden flower known for its pure white petals, its great size and the yellow centre. The American creator was Luther Burbank, and he named this showy bloom after the snow topped Mount Shasta, or White Mountain as seen from his home in California.

Burdock *Arctium Lappa*

The Latin name is very descriptive of the fruits of this plant. Arctium means 'bear', and lappa 'to seize'. The barbed, round seed ball easily attaches itself to the coats of animals and humans alike.

The roots and seeds are the useful part, and in the war years it was collected for its use in medicines. It is described as a blood purifier. The burdock root has been used to aid skin and rheumatic complaints. There is an impressive list of ailments that it was reported to help and it has been used by Culpeper, the Chinese, the Native Americans and the Shakers.

The burdock has the most enormous leaves, and it prefers the shadier parts of the churchyard. Its barbed seed heads are a menace. Instead of being infuriated by the inconvenience of de-barbing himself and his dog, Swiss electrical engineer George de Mestral took a serious look at the mechanics of the hooking device. In 1941 he invented Velcro! Nature can teach so much. Mestral named his invention after Velvet and Crochet, the hook and loop system. Velcro has pretty well transformed our lives, items of clothing and footwear, especially for the young making it easier to get dressed.

Mestral was not the first one to see the opportunities of the grabbing burr seed head.

There is a custom seemingly going back to the 12th century which involves covering a volunteer from head to toe with the green burrs. He is known as the Burry Man. This odd tradition takes place on the second Friday in August. The Burry Man is then taken around all the public houses and treated to beer through a straw for the entire day. He has two supporters, as he is completely inflexible in this costume, especially to bear the weight of his outstretched arms. This takes place in the small town of Queensferry, outside of Edinburgh.

Knapweed *Centaurea nigra*

This is a later flowering plant in the grassy area at the east side of the churchyard. It seems a popular plant with the many butterflies I have seen feeding on the purple heads.

Once upon a time it was used to stop nose bleeds. The old herbalists used it to treat running sores, both cancerous and fistulas.

Knapweed is known as a vulnerary, a plant used in wound healing.

Mugwort *Artemisia vulgaris*

Mugwort it is suggested likes to grow by a hedge, in this case the one growing in the churchyard had availed itself of the south and the west hedges, nestled in the corner, surrounded by hedge woundwort.

As for women, this is an excellent choice of herb to aid the delivery of a baby and the afterbirth, (if the mother lived in Culpeper's day). Now it might be suggested for menstrual problems, but professional help on the matter should be sought.

Dandelion *Taraxacum officinale*

The dandelion has the power to strongly divide opinions. Loved by the artist and herbalist, and loathed by the gardener.

To the artist the fabulously intricate 'clock' of the dandelion is quite exquisite and often seen in a painting or as a piece of sculpture. It can be exciting to blow the head and watch the little seeded parachutes sail into the blue yonder. Many children do just that without any knowledge of what their innocent actions can precipitate.

To the committed gardener however, it is the worse horror that can befall the manicured lawn. Herbicide commercials often show the hapless dandelion as the villain of the piece!

Let's consider the gardeners. They have a right to be concerned. The greedy tap root of the dandelion takes three times as much iron out of the soil than other plants, and in return exhales ethylene gas. The best use a gardener can make of them is in the compost heap where eventually the nutritional benefits will enrich other more desired plants.

Therefore the plant is rich in many nutrients, it is said to contain more vitamin C and A than any other vegetable or fruit, and of much value as a plant medicine.

Over a century ago before the manufacture of weed killers, the New York Parks Department hit upon an idea to get rid of the troublesome dandelions. European immigrants were invited in to help themselves to dandelions. This custom was written about by Mrs Earle in her books about the settlers to the USA. She describes hundreds of gaily dressed women and children from the Italian and Portuguese communities having a day gathering leaves, digging out the roots, and collecting the flowers. The flowers would be turned into beer or wine, the leaves for salads, and the roots dried, roasted and ground down to make a coffee type beverage.

However, a hundred years later Steve Brill, a promoter of free food was arrested on March 29, 1986, by two undercover park rangers who had infiltrated his Central Park tour. He was handcuffed for eating a dandelion. The police fingerprinted Brill and charged him with criminal mischief for removing vegetation from the park, but Brill had eaten the evidence, so they released him with a desk-appearance ticket pending trial. Brill has capitalised on his fame, and is a great champion of healthy eating, and using plants as medicine.

Tinctures of dandelion are used as a digestive bitter, to promote the appetite. This acts as a choleretic, which aids the production of bile. It is also a liver tonic, and is a diuretic.

The diuretic notion lived on into my childhood, it was known to youngsters as 'pee the bed'! It must have been effective, otherwise why would this old name prevail?

And finally as dandelions are related to time and clocks…

> "The clock is running. Make the most of today. Time waits for no man. Yesterday is history. Tomorrow is a mystery. Today is a gift. That's why it is called the present."

> – Alice Morse Earle

Cat's ear *Hypochaeris radicata*

Cat's ear can be used in the same way as the dandelion.

A few summers ago, a collection of yellow headed dandelion type of plant took over the section of land between the old graves and the front of the church. Whilst I am a passionate fan of the plants, on this occasion, even I could see that it was not a 'good look'. The volunteer gardeners do a terrific job of caring for the churchyard, and the area they particularly concentrate on are the newer graves. Many of the plants behaved like the thugs that they are usually portrayed to be. The 'cute' seed heads were running amok (perhaps floating amok), seeding and producing more plants. On one particularly dull Saturday it was not a pretty site. So, what was in this collection?

Goat's beard *Tragopogon pratensis*

Also know as noon flower, Jack-go-to-bed-at noon

This is a rather handsome plant, if one looks down onto the flower, it is a perfectly arranged head, unlike the untidy look of the dandelion. There is a rather attractive bulbous shape supporting the flower head. Gerard writes of this plant favourably, he describes the purple version found in the north of England, down south we have the yellow variety. It is no longer regarded as the medicinal plant it once was. Gerard almost celebrates the ability of this plant when maturity is reached, "Yhey grow into a downy Blowball like those of dandelion, which is carried away by the wind." It is said that the bulbs were eaten like parsnips.

Bristly ox tongue *Helminthotheca echioides*

Also known as Lang de boeuf

The whole plant could be made as a decoction and used as a de-obstructant, according to Culpeper. It is a close relative of goat's beard.

Perennial Sow-Thistle *Sonchus arvensis*
Smooth Sow Thistle *Sonchus oleraceus*

Also known as hare's thistle, hare's lettuce

Both sow thistles can be used for fevers, urinary disorders, stomach complaints, stone, deafness, inflammation, swelling and haemorrhoids. Gerard said that "the juice of these herbs doth cool and temper the heat of the fundament and privy parts." It was also recommended for those that were short-winded and troubled by wheezing.

Today they are rarely used, and only as a poultice for swellings, particularly boils.

Hawkweeds *Hieracium aug.*
Hawkbits *Leontodon hispidus*
Hawksbeard smooth *Crepis capillaris*

Those plants seem interchangeable, in Tudor times they might be used for decongestion of the lungs. They may have eased coughs. Today they are little used.

Thistles

Thistles are a very handsome group of plants.

The four varieties found in the churchyard are:

Spear thistle *Cirsium vulgare*
Creeping thistle *Cirsium arvense*
Woolly thistle *Cirsium eriophorum*
Slender thistle *Carduus tenuiflorus*

The medicinal part of the plants are the roots and leaves. Mrs Grieve states that the ancients had used this plant as a specific in the treatment of cancer, the juice could be used to treat cancer and ulcers.

Culpeper suggested the juice for cricks in the neck, and good for children suffering from rickets.

Thistles were found almost everywhere in the churchyard.

Borgainaceae

Forget-me-not *Myosotis symphytifolia*

According to Mrs Grieve, "it has a strong affinity for the respiratory organs, especially the left lower lung. On the Continent it is sometimes made into a syrup and given for pulmonary problems. There is a tradition that a decoction or juice of the plants hardens steel."

Forget-me-not was found growing in the gravel path of the churchyard.

When I was a child I discovered forget-me-not, and thought that it would add something to my Uncle's beloved rose garden. To me there were just too many bits of bare earth that needed covering. It didn't take long for the forget-me-not to crowd the roses out. I was too young to realise that roses like space to themselves.

Brassicaceae – Cabbage Family

Charlock *Sinapis arvensis*

Also known as wild mustard

In amongst the old graves there was such a profusion of plants, sometimes difficult to see what was there. This was the case with charlock, and only when checking the photographs on the computer did I have a close up of this bold plant, dark green leaves and smallish yellow flowers. I had a closer look on the next visit and found it. Mustard was invaluable to our ancestors for spicing up bland food and making it more palatable. Its seeds were not the best of the mustards, but acceptable. Once upon a time I heard mention of 'mustard plasters' and guess they were used by my grandparents. This would have eased congestion on the chest, especially with coughs, colds and flu. A basin of hot water and mustard was used to help rid a person of a cold.

This is the 'mustard' that forms one of the 38 Bach Flower Remedies

Shepherd's Purse *Capsella bursa-pastoris*

Shepherd's Purse had a great many other names, most referring to the 'purse', which is this plant's distinguishing feature. It grows about 40cm tall, has uninteresting dull white flowers, and lots of little purses of seeds.

Traditionally has been known as having styptic, haemostatic or astringent qualities, which can arrest bleeding, both internally and externally. This is just one of many plants with this quality, and was sought out as treatment for wounds on battle fields, certainly during the First World War. Shepherd's Purse is also of value for 'women's' problems.

Shepherd's purse was used to treat diarrhoea too.

In more recent years shepherd's purse has been 'rediscovered' as a treatment for prolapses of the rectum, uterus and bladder, and muscular atrophy. This revelation is attributed to the famous herbalist Maria Treben. In the 1980s her books on herbal cures were well regarded. She used the traditional German/Eastern European remedies that had been proven to work for many generations of people.

An elderly gentleman gifted Treben an old book of herbs, and looking through this she spotted an entry on shepherd's purse and made the discovery about the treatment for prolapse and atrophy. Within a short time, she was putting the cure to the test, with seemingly excellent results.

Common whitlow grass *Erophila verna*

Common whitlow grass plant was completely new to me. Early one spring I spotted a patch of what looked like confetti, and on closer inspection discovered minute flower-heads in the grass. The plant resembled chickweed, but far too small. It had four deeply indented white petals.

Friends Iris and Audrey helped search through books for answers, but none were found. Sometime later I stumbled upon an artist's impression that showed me clearly what it was. As to what it might treat, the answer is in the name!

Today one rarely hears of whitlow, also known as felon. It was an infection that formed on the side of the finger nail, and could result in swelling, redness and a gathering of fluid. This would have been extremely painful, and the resulting poison would have caused malaise. Today this would be treated with antibiotics.

Cuckoo flower *Cardamine pratensis*

Cuckoo flower is also known as milkmaid and lady's smock. It shows its pretty four petals of white or pinky-purple at the time the cuckoo is heard.; and often grows in damp places. There are superstitions attached to picking it. The first that it will provoke a thunderstorm, the other that the person will attract adders, and at some stage in the following year an adder will bite. Actually, I did pick one flower to press (in the interest of furthering my knowledge). It was going to be mown some days later, therefore justifying my action. That was quite a few years ago, and so far I have fortunately avoided snakes.

Obviously not everyone believed the superstition, as the foliage was used in the same way as watercress, and was a tasty addition the salads of long ago.

In the olden days it was used to 'provoke' the urine, break the stone and aid digestion. It was also regarded as good treatment for scurvy. Today it is known that the plant contains vitamin C therefore substantiating the claim that it was useful for that condition.

Shakespeare mentions lady's smock in Love's Labour Lost:

> "When daisies pied and violets blue
> And lady-smocks all silver white,
> And cuckoo-buds of yellow hue,
> Do paint the meadows with delight…"

> – Act V, scene 11

Garlic Mustard *Alliaria petiolata*

Also known as hedge garlic, Jack-by-the-hedge, sauce-all-alone, poor man's mustard.

The herbalist William Coles wrote in 1657 that garlic mustard was eaten by country people as a sauce to their "Salt-fish, an helpeth well to digest the crudities, and other crude humors that are engendered by the eating thereof."

Early herbalists used Garlic Mustard to treat dropsy and to induce sweating. Sir John Hill in his book *The Family Herbal* suggested that it should be boiled with honey to make a syrup as a treatment for coughs and hoarseness. The leaves were thought to have antiseptic properties, and applied to open sores as a dressings. It can be used as a condiment. It is found under the hedges.

Caprifoliaceae

Elder *Sambucus nigra*

In times gone by this tree was much revered as it was regarded as the medical chest of the country, and a few sentences here cannot do this wonderful plant justice.

Folk in the old days would use the flower-heads as an insect repellent, and would hang bunches over the horses pulling carts to rid them of flies. The flowers were used with Vaseline to make hand cream. Elderflower tea in early spring could reduce the symptoms of hay fever. The flowers had pain-killing properties, could induce sweating, and could also bring down a fever. On an indulgent note, the flowers can be steeped in vodka to make a rather good cordial, and like the sloe, a very welcome winter drink. With just a little honey it is an excellent 'pick me up'. The berries can help with the winter ailments, colds, flu and sore throats. The berries are a great source of vitamin C.

Other uses: the berries can be made into dye and ink. The leaves can be used in an ointment for sprains and strains. Recent research has found that the flowers have an antiviral action against Herpes Simplex type 1.

Honeysuckle *Lonicera periclymenum*

Also known as Woodbine.

Honeysuckle is said to have been one of the first flowers to be given a name in the 8th century; its scent is a sweet delight! It is odd to think that flowers were not named, but in fact nothing was named. It was to be a few centuries before birds, butterflies and clouds were given names.

In Culpeper's day, the leaves of honeysuckle were used as gargles for sore throats; to relieve a cough, and as a means to open obstructions of the liver and spleen. Today's herbalists might use it as a laxative or emetic. It is reputed to increase sweating which might be useful in ridding the body of toxic substances.

The flowers may be used for respiratory problems, coughs, catarrh and asthma.

Honeysuckle is said to contain natural antibiotics and salicylic acid. Salicylic acid is also found in willow and meadowsweet. Salicylic acid is the template for the drug aspirin, so herbalists might use the honeysuckle for colds, flu, fevers aches and pains, rheumatism, arthritis and headache.

Caryophyllaceae

Red campion *Silene dioica*
White campion *Silene latifolia*

Both campions can claim fame as a soap. By boiling up the root water, a housewife had a means of getting her washing clean. Cleanliness is important to good health! Both are found by the hedge in the west of the church.

Red campion has been used in recent times as a constituent in the Phytobiophysics Flower Formulas. Like the Bach Flower Remedies, they contribute to the wellbeing of the individual's 'Spiritual Ease". In modern times there is much need for spiritual ease.

Greater stitchwort *Stellaria holostea*

This is a pretty and delicate plant that grows among the old graves. As its Latin name suggests it has a white star-like flower.

The name has nothing to do with sewing, but according to herbalist William Coles, this plant is used for… what else? …stitches.

A stitch is the catching pain at the side, following a period of exertion.

Chickweed *Stellaria media*

Chickweed gets its name from the little white flower that looks like a star, (stella), also the fact that it is beloved of chickens. It is seen growing almost all year round. Humans enjoy chickweed as a spring green, it can be used as a salad leaf, or cooked with butter. It makes a good broth to help those recovering from illness. Chickweed might even be used as a slimming preparation. It is said to work either by the 'saponins' dissolving the body fat, or by increasing urination. American herbalist, the aptly named Susan Weed, says of chickweed, when used internally 'it sponges up the spills' and 'tidies up the rips', saying of it that it 'has deep mending skills'.

In herbal medicine it is known as a treatment for rheumatism, chest infections, gastritis, colitis, acid indigestion and IBS.

More particularly it is associated with skin problems. It is known as a 'refrigerant', as it has the ability to cool hot, inflamed skin conditions such as eczema and sun burn. It is reputed to help with itching, urticaria, ulcers, abscess, varicose veins, psoriasis, spots and boils. Chickweed is said to have cell-proliferant properties, which can speed up the healing of a wound.

In recent years two mothers, living in the south of England, were distraught at having to watch their children suffering from distressing eczema. Independently of each other they took to creating a soothing cream for their children. Working from herbals, they collected a few plants as suggested in the books and spent time concocting a cream. Both were successful, and improved the condition of their children. Friends and neighbours also endorsed the value of the creams, and this attracted the attention of the media.

Natalie Balmond experimented with beeswax, nettle, CHICKWEED, and chamomile. Her preparation was a success, and she has turned it into a business. Her ointment is available on the NHS.

Tracy Wood used marigold, CHICKWEED, and vegetable oil, along with a few other ingredients. Her success took her to being a finalist in Female Inventor of the Year in 2001.

It has to be said that there are many causes of eczema, diet, lifestyle, stress and emotional issues, all these things need to be considered too.

Clusiaceae

St John's wort *Hypericum perforatum*

This plant takes its name from John the Baptist, as it flowers around the 24th June, which is sometimes known as Johnsmass. It is a time of long summer evenings. I found it at that time of year standing proudly amid the other summer flowering plants in the middle of the old graves.

In the 1990s St. John's wort burst onto the scene as a treatment for SAD, (seasonally affected disorder), and seemed to bring a measure of relief to those people who suffered from a lack of sunshine in the winter months. Since then it has gained a reputation as a means of treating depression and anxiety.

There are a good number of clinical trials showing that St. John's wort can alleviate anxiety and insomnia, and it appears to be an effective treatment. It has high concentration of hypericin which acts as a sedative and calms nerves, with fewer side effects than drugs. The BMJ has urged doctors to prescribe St. John's wort for mild to moderate depression.

St John's Wort does have other uses. An herbalist might use St. John's wort externally for bruises, burns, wounds, neurological pain, sciatica and rheumatics.

Used internally, it is said to be a powerful antiviral. Research now shows that there is a possibility that the active ingredients contained within the plant might be useful in tackling the multiplication of viruses (retroviruses). Much clinical work is being done currently on this study.

Convolvulaceae

Field bindweed *Convolvulus arvensis*

The petite pink and white field bindweed romps innocently along the ground. Quite adorable, that is unless you are a gardener. According to Mea Allen in her book *Weeds* this little chap can cover an area of 30 square yards in a season. In my own garden I battle hard to get rid of it.

Hedge bindweed *Calystegia sepium*

Without a doubt this is a very handsome plant. It is related to the showy and narcotic morning glory. In spite of being beautiful it has the ability to lovingly strangle other cherished plants.

Both the above were found at the south side, by, and in the hedge. The they both have purgative qualities.

Crassulaceae

Orpine *Sedum telephium*

It is difficult to be absolutely certain of what a plant might be without ever seeing it in flower. There are no other sedums in the churchyard that I have come across. The leaves of this plant meet the size and shape of the Orpine.

Culpeper writes that the bruised leaves applied to wounds will heal them, and the Celts before him also used Orpine for inflamed wounds.

Recently I met an Italian lady who told me of an incident when she was a girl During WW11 when Northern Italy was occupied by the Germans, Carmela was sent out with a message under cover of darkness.

She stepped into a roll of barbed wire, that had not been there earlier. Carmela was found later and helped out of the wire, but her legs were badly damaged.

A local woman went into the mountains to find a special leaf. From the description it sounded very like Orpine. It took time, but eventually Carmela's legs healed.

Cucurbitaceae

White bryony *Bryonia dioica*

White bryony is a climbing plant with handsomely structured leaves and tendrils. The berries are orange or red, and poisonous. It has inspired stone and wood carvers, and examples can be seen in a number of churches and cathedrals. White bryony belongs to the Cucurbitaceae family, and related to marrows and squashes, melons and pumpkins.

This was a plant that I had not met before. It is to be found under the large yew tree on the south side of the church. There is little for it to climb on so it scrambles along the ground to find the light, and spills onto the lawn. It is probable that the stone-masons used the leaf as a template for the carved features inside the church.

Culpepper used white bryony to treat many ailments, but he did warn that "The root of bryony purges the belly with great violence, troubling the stomach and burning the liver and therefore not rashly to be taken." Dr William Withering used the boiled root as a purge for cattle.

White bryony was thought to be an antidote to leprosy. The whole plant has an antiviral effect.

Today it would only be used by medical herbalists, and given in minute doses for chest complaints, rheumatism and gout; or by homeopaths in even smaller doses to bring relief to those suffering bronchitis, sciatica and arthritis.

The large root of the white bryony was sometimes moulded underground so that it resembled the magical and highly prized 'mandrake'. This root resembled the shape of a human, thereby it held enormous powers for good and evil. This sculptured piece could fetch quite a price from the unwary.

Charles Darwin was intrigued by the climbing habit of the plant. During a storm he watched its upward progress, thus observing the tip of the tendril reaching up, the rest of the tendril tightening into a spiral, then pulling the stem upwards. The tendril straightened itself and proceeded to coil in the opposite direction, which held it fast to the support tree.

It was said that Caesar wore a wreath of white bryony to protect himself from lightning.

Dioscoreaceae

Black bryony *Tamus communis*

Over many years of observation, I noticed what I thought was a rather sinister plant. It appeared in the south west corner of the graveyard. I was aware that it produced a single stem which was quickly united with others before it raced off to embed itself into the hedge. One spring I made a study of it. From a grave a small snakelike head appeared (which happened to the single leaf). It was more brown in tone than green, and was quickly followed by another. The two garnered support from each other, and they became stronger. Their speed of growth demonstrated the Fibonacci principle perfectly. In no time the hedge had been reached by the two leaders, closely followed by others. The flowers were fairly insignificant, but the joy of the plant was the berries. The black bryony wound its way in circular fashion through the hedge, and much later in the year when the leaves had withered a garland of red berries were left. So pretty. It was something I'd noticed in the woods, but thought that the berries might have belonged to the shrub, and to be honest, I hadn't really looked closely.

The black bryony is distantly related to the white bryony. It belongs to the Dioscoreaceae family, and they don't resemble each other in looks. The leaves of the black bryony are heart shaped, very dark green and shiny. As the year advances some leaves take on a bronze sheen. The berries are bright red, and are poisonous. It is a handsome plant, even although it is regarded a garden pest.

Medicinally it proved to be a powerful diuretic. Externally the pulp was used as a plaster to relieve the pain of gout and rheumatism, and was of use to those suffering paralysis. A tincture of the root seemed useful to relieve the discomfort of unbroken chilblains.

Black bryony is rarely used today.

Dipsacaceae

Scabious field *Knautia arvensis*

This I found on the north side of the church, but at the east end, so it was benefiting from some sunshine. This was under the lime trees, and well to the right of the 'thugs' in the area, no thorns, hooks or stinging bits to it. It stood out with its bluish-lilac florets.

Its name is a bit unfortunate, Scabious suggests a scab, a scaly sore, which comes from scabies, which was a form of leprosy. Therefore, it was known for what it could treat in the olden days.

The generic name *knautia* is from the Saxon doctor, Knaut.

Many little girls are named after pretty plants. This is a pretty plant, but blighted by its given name.

Equisetaceae

Horsetail *Equestum arvense*

Also known as shave-grass, bottle-brush, pewterwort

The horsetail family are something of a one off. They are not related to any other plant, and can be traced back to the carboniferous period. In times gone by the horsetail could be employed as cure for internal ulcers, fresh wounds, and ruptures in children.

In modern times it is used in some USA Medical Centres to stop bleeding, heal ulcers, and treat kidney problems. The plant contains silica, much needed for the good condition of hair and nails.

The name pewterwort gives an idea of how it would have been used by the housemaid of old, it makes a great scouring pad, long before the benefits of steel wool !

Horsetail frequently grows around the edges of fields, the one I found had made it into the churchyard. In fields about two miles away, close to running water the horsetail is of giant proportion. They look positively prehistoric, and I guess they are.

Euphorbia

Dog's mercury *Mercurialis perennis*

Culpeper roundly states that there is "not a more fatal plant than this." He is critical of Gerard and Parkinson for not cautioning their readers against the use of this plant. It is used in homeopathy, in obviously very, very dilute amounts. It is used to treat problems of the gall bladder and liver. It can alleviate rheumatism, and stop diarrhoea.

Dog's Mercury is to be found is in ancient woodlands.

Fabaceae - Clovers

Red clover *Trifolium pratense*

Clovers on account of their three leaves, are plants of symbolism. To the Druids the leaves represented the earth, the sea and the heavens. St Patrick used the plant to explain the Holy Trinity, while other beliefs suggest it represents faith, hope and charity, and should there be a fourth leaf, it represented Good Luck. In the wake of St Patrick, the shamrock became the national flower of Ireland.

In herbal medicine clover is used as a good spring tonic. It can rid the body of toxins by increasing the flow of urine. It can clear the lungs of mucous, and it is also used as a mild laxative.

Clover today is also useful to women, the flavonoid content is oestrogen like, and is said to help maintain a normal oestrogen level during the menopause. It can help with the usual problems at this stage in life, and it is also thought it could help prevent osteoporosis.

There are claims that red clover is useful in the treatment of cancer, and indeed has been used as components in Harry Hoxsey and Rene Caisse's herbal treatments. It has been claimed that tumours can be reduced by using the Red clover herbal tea. Today trials are ongoing.

It provides the bees with the material to make a very fine honey.

White clover *Trifolium repens*

Also known as Dutch clover

The white clover seems to be much less useful than the red variety. Here are a few of its uses. It was once used to treat coughs, colds and fevers. It is said to be of use if bitten by venomous beasts! Modern herbalists prefer to use the red clover.

In the days before commercial fertilisers the value of clover was recognised as a means of introducing nitrogen to the soil, therefore it was ploughed in, and would thus improve the quality of any crops planted.

Black medick *Medicago lupulina*

This little yellow plant like the two above grows in the area of the old graves. It is small and more ground hugging. Rarely used today, it was said to have been used as a laxative.

In modern times there is a great focus on the more emotional problems, which so often are the underlying causes of physical illness. It is used in Phytobiophysics Flower Formulas for 'Relaxation'.

Birdsfoot trefoil *Lotus corniculatus*

This is another plant used in the Phytobiophysical Formulas. Together with other herbal plants, can alleviate low self esteem. The Phytobiophysics are a relative new treatment, and cannot be fully explored in a such a short piece of text.

The following two do not have any known medicinal qualities, but they are pretty, and the meadow needs such plants. They too are likely providers of nitrogen.

Tufted vetch *Vicia cracca*
Meadow vetchling *Lathyrus pratensis*

Geraniaceae

Herb Robert *Geranium robertianum*

Herb robert I have loved from my earliest years. I knew that if I pinched the leaves it would release an aroma which pleased me, others would not agree, and call it an 'odour'.

The distinctive colours and composition of the plant please me too, therefore a great favourite, even in my garden.

Herb robert often known as crane's bill due to the shape of the seed pod, which, (other than the strange scent) made it easily recognisable. Its name came from the founder of the Cistercian order in the 11th century, Abbe Robert. In the Medieval times herb robert was used to ward off evil spirits and ill health, but it does in fact have a great many uses.

This plant was much loved by Culpeper as a means of dealing with problems of bleeding. In the case of accidents, the crushed leaves can be applied to the wound to cause the bleeding to cease. Today an herbalist might use this plant to deal with peptic ulcers and internal bleeding. It can be used as a gargle for the mouth and throat. It is said that a tea made from herb robert can lower blood sugar in diabetes.

There are claims that herb robert can astringe 'out of control' muscles, which means that conditions such as stress incontinence and prolapse can be improved with herbal tea of the herb robert.

Herb robert is often used in homeopathy. It is thought of as a cancer cure in Scottish folk medicine.

Meadow crane's bill *Geranium pratense*

This plant was used as a treatment for wounds. Meadow crane's bill has also been used to bring reduce fevers, kill pain and reduce inflammation.

Dove's foot *Geranium molle*

It has similar properties to the meadow variety. Culpeper had a few uses for it, including internal bruises, getting rid of stones in the kidneys and for cleaning old sores. Today the American wild crane's bill would be used instead.

Gramineae – Grasses

Couch grass *Agropyron repens*

Also known as twitch grass, scutch, dog's grass, quick grass.

Couch grass is a loathsome thing to gardeners. The rhizomes run underground, and unless every bit is removed from the soil, it will sprout up again. It is often necessary to clear the whole flower bed and leave for a while to be sure that every piece has been removed.

However, this troublesome rhizome has some medicinal value. It can be unearthed in the spring or early autumn, washed and dried carefully, then prepared as a decoction. This involves boiling a small quantity of the rhizome for ten minutes, to make a tea. The main uses that an herbalist might put this plant to concern the treatment of problems of the urinary system, cystitis, urethritis and prostatitis. All of these conditions have inflammation, as suggested by the

'-itis'. Couch Grass has demulcent properties which can soothe the irritation and deal with the inflammation. It may also be used in the case of kidney stones. So, for anyone suffering the above, it is a very useful plant.

Oat *Avena sativa*

Oats have been part of modern man's diet since the early days of farming. In Tudor times the oats cooked with salt might have been used to relieve the pain of a stitch.

In the past it was popular in skin care, used as a face pack to improve the skin, or put in a bath to soften the water, preferably in a cloth bag. Oats are still used in soaps and creams.

Commonly used as a breakfast cereal, oats are a nervine, calming to the nerves and promoted as such today.

Barley *Hordeum distichon*

The part used is the grain, known as pearl barley. The medicinal qualities of the plant are useful in the treatment of urinary tract infections, and respiratory problems.

It was used in broth which was a staple once upon a time, and it must have had a positive effect on the health.

Malt is a by-product in the making of beer and whisky. This horrid sticky stuff was once used as a 'tonic' and administered daily to growing children. It might have been nicer to take if it was given in milk! Malt was used in popular bedtime drinks such as Horlicks and Ovaltine.

Today the green barley is made into a health giving superfood.

Barley and oats were found inside the hedge on the south west side of the churchyard. It is hardly surprising to find some as the fields round about are arable.

Iridaceae

Gladwyn *Iris foetidissima*

The common name gladwyn meaning 'sword-grass' comes from its sword like leaves. It is reputed to smell unpleasant, thus earning it the name 'stinking gladwyn'.

This member of the iris family is much shorter than its showy cousin, the flower is pale mauve, and slightly greyish in colour. In the autumn when it reveals its seeds it is transformed into an eye catching display of orange.

In ancient times the Greek physicians used this iris, together with honey for chest complaints such as bronchitis.

Poultices of the crushed leaves were used to draw out arrowheads, and other foreign bodies like splinters of wood from the flesh.

Some herbalists today might use the iris to alleviate migraines.

Lamiaceae – Dead nettles and mints

Wild marjoram *Origanum vulgare*

A few years ago when sitting among the wildflowers in the oldest part of the churchyard, I decided to write about the healing herbs that I happened to find. There was a profusion of beautiful coloured flowers, with marjoram being one of them. These flowers were being visited by many winged creatures, including bees. Marjoram is known as a 'bee plant'.

Finding marjoram growing on a grave was seemingly significant. In the old days powdered marjoram was sprinkled in the winding sheet used at burials. To later find marjoram growing on the grave indicated that the dearly departed loved one was happy in the after life, thus bringing comfort to the deceased.

Our ancestors benefited in many ways from this useful plant. In the home it would be used as a strewing herb. It was used to scour wooden furniture to clean and prevent woodworm. It made the washing water agreeably sweet and to make potpourri. As a dye it coloured woollen cloth light purple, and linen would turn a reddish brown.

Country folk might gather bundles of marjoram to hang in their cottages to provide 'tea', and also for use as a flavouring for the home brew, before hops became fashionable.

Marjoram has many healing uses, for instance for the elderly, it has anti-ageing properties. It helps with degenerative arthritis; helps with osteoarthritis and rheumatism, and can contribute to general good health.

For those with respiratory problems, herbalists use marjoram for bronchitis, asthma and coughs. For digestive problems, marjoram can relieve indigestion and dyspepsia. marjoram can be used externally as a fomentation for painful swellings and rheumatism.

Marjoram is used mainly as a culinary herb, but the plant can also yield a volatile oil. This oil can be used in aromatherapy, and in fact clinical trials were carried out in a London hospital to prove that patients suffering high blood pressure could experience a lower, more normal level of blood pressure which would last for quite a few days after a massage.

The scientific name for marjoram is *origanum* which is taken from the Greek words 'oros' meaning mountain, and 'ganos' meaning joy, therefore it is known as 'Joy of the Mountains'. In Grecian and Roman times garlands of marjoram were worn on the heads of newly married couples.

It is indeed a joyful and useful plant to behold in the churchyard.

Wild basil *Clinopodium vulgare*

Also known as hedge basil, hedge calamint

Identifying this plant proved problematic. It appeared to be from the mint family, and the Latin name suggests it is.

A number of books were needed to find the correct definition. which turned out to be wild basil ! A long lanky plant that seemed more inclined to lie along the ground, and only the top bit managing to head skywards It appeared to be a weak plant, but a survivor.

Wild basil does have its place, as a heart stimulant, as an aid to improve digestion, and can prevent flatulence.

Self heal *Prunella vulgaris*

Self Heal is a member of the mint family. This plant might be used today as an astringent gargle for sore throats and a mouthwash for ulcers and bleeding gums. It is a treatment that goes back to the days when brunella (as it was known in Germany) was used by garrisoned soldiers for inflammatory mouth and throat problems. This use persisted until about seventy years ago.

Self heal like the yarrow could be claimed to be the herb of the carpenters, as it was used to heal wounds caused by sharp wood-working tools. It is also known as 'siclewort' coming from a time when most country folk would be busy bringing in the harvest and likely to injure themselves from an overly sharp sickle.

Gerard said of self heal, "There is not a better wounde herbe in the world," and a century later Culpeper claimed that the plant got its name because "When you are hurt, you may heal yourself."

Up until the Second World War self heal was being used to staunch bleeding and a treatment for heart disease.

Herbalists may also use self heal to treat headaches related to tension.

The recent edition of *Potter's Herbal* reports that anti-inflammatory and anti-allergic activity has been observed, and states that self heal is used as an anti-cancer drug in China.

Self heal proliferated in the whole churchyard

Black horehound *Ballota nigra*

This plant certainly looks like a member of the nettle family. It was reputed to be the cure for the bites of mad dogs, and had at the ability to clean foul ulcers. If one suffered from worms, then this plant might just be the thing to clear them from the system. Today it is still recognised as a vermifuge, which is a plant that will rid the body of worms. Black horehound can lower the blood pressure. It has stood the test of time. It is another plant happy amongst the old graves.

Hedge Woundwort *Stachys sylvatica*

Hedge woundwort is abundant in the shady sites, in this case it occupied the corner at the south west of the churchyard.

It is quite a pretty purple/pink flower and can be half a metre tall. The name suggests its uses as an herb; wound wart for wounds and cuts, and stachys, a Latinised Greek word meaning spike. It is a styptic, and one can understand that it would have been sought out after a battle. Recent research confirms that the plant can not only staunch bleeding, but has an antiseptic property. Useful to know if one is out in the countryside and have the misfortune to cut oneself. The leaf applied to the wound directly will cause the bleeding to cease, and will clean the wound at the same time.

Thomas Green, author of *The Universal Herbal* (1832) says this of Woundwort – "Toads are thought to be fond of living under its shade." Woundwort it also known to attract bees.

Woundwort can produce a yellow dye, and the stems like those of the nettle and flax could be used as a fibre.

Archangel *Lamium album*

Also known as white dead nettle, Adam & Eve

Archangel, unlike the stinging nettle, does not sting! In fact, it is not even a nettle, but belongs to the mint family. It grows alongside the nettle. The term 'dead' indicates that it will not cause any physical harm. It can be fun to demonstrate bravery by grasping it in the full knowledge that it will not hurt.

Archangel flowers around the 8th of May, the feast day of the Archangel Michael.

Folklore suggests that the Archangel is lucky for lovers, and by turning the plant upside down it shows the stamens within the flower resembling a couple lying side by side in a canopied bed.

It is said that the leaves are delicious cooked with butter.

Archangel does not have the many properties of the stinging nettle, but has a few of its own. In Culpeper's time it was used against quartan agues, this term means a fever recurring every fourth day, both days of consecutive occurrence being counted.

It could staunch bleeding of the nose and mouth; relieve the pains of gout and sciatica; healing old wounds and ulcers, and regulate menstruation.

Today's herbalist will still use the plant for menstrual problems, and for prostatitis in men. It can stimulate the liver and help relieve catarrhal conditions.

Red dead nettle *Lamium purpureum*

This plant too was known as Archangel, but the fact that it was red in colour suggested to the herbalists of old that it was good for conditions of the blood. This plant is said to boost the immune system, due to its vitamin C and the flavonoid quercetin content. The red dead nettle has also been found to be effective against E.coli bacteria. It is quite a pretty plant too.

Red dead nettle is valuable to bee keepers as an early forage plant for the emerging bees.

Henbit *Lamium amplexicaule*

Henbit is a smaller plant. The slender rose coloured flowers are more pronounced that those of the purple dead nettle.

Both plants are used to arrest bleeding.

Ground ivy *Glechoma hederacae*

Ground ivy has dark green leaves and a very pretty mauve flower. In olden days images of this plant were used to decorate the signs at hostelries and taverns, as it was used to clarify and add flavour to ale. This earned it the name 'alehoof'.

The plant itself has less likeable qualities. It likes to spread, and indeed makes room for itself by crowding out the opposition, therefore it is unloved by gardeners and farmers. Ground Ivy contains a number of nutrients, nitrogen, tannins, choline, silica and mineral salts.

Many notable herbalists from the past used ground ivy, including the Greek Galen for inflamed eyes and Gerard for 'ringing of the ears', better known as tinnitus. In the past it was a useful plant to have growing around the home in the winter as it is known to relieve many winter ailments, bronchitis, colds, catarrh and congestion.

Bugle *Ajuga reptans*

Also known as sickle wort, herb carpenter

In the time of Culpeper this plant should have been in everyone's medicine chest. It was particularly useful as a treatment for internal bruising, ulcers and sores, and claimed to cure problems of the mouth and gums, and other 'secret places' of men and women.

Today it is regarded as an astringent, and can be used for internal bleeding, just as in Culpeper's day. The bugle in the churchyard was not particularly tall, it was generally smothered by all the competing plants around the old graves.

Malvaceae – Mallows

Common mallow *Malva sylvestris*

After the show of dandelions along the roadsides and footpaths there comes the pretty mauve/pink flowered mallow. It goes on to flower most of the summer.

In the 16th century the mallow was known as omnimorbia, a 'cure-all'. Further back in time the Romans grew the mallow for its medicinal qualities and indeed the Roman scholar Pliny suggested taking a sip of mallow juice daily to ward off illness.

In recent years the herbalist Thomas Bartram recommended the common mallow for the following: respiratory ailments and the common cold; coughs and bronchial irritation; and inflammation of the throat or mouth.

The roots and branches are both efficacious. They work well being stewed and applied to all sorts of wounds. It is said to heal all manner of swellings.

In past times children enjoy stringing up the seeds of the mallow like beads. They call the seeds cheeses.

Musk mallow *Malva moschata*

The musk seems to prefer the open site beyond the church in the grassy area. It is regarded as a more elegant flower than the Common Mallow, and has a musky scent. It has a paler pink flower, and more indented leaf. Musk mallow has the same qualities as the common mallow, but is less potent.

Onagraceae

Rosebay willow-herb *Chamerion angustifolium*

Also known as fireweed.

This tall, handsome, pink plant would not look out of place

in the garden, but its beauty is only skin deep! It has a root structure that can rampage through the soil, and new shoots spring up at some distance from the main plant. The seeds descend by parachute into the welcoming soil, therefore it has been classed as a nuisance, and a WEED. A single plant can send forth 80,000 seed parachutes.

The name 'fireweed' refers to its preference for ground that has been recently burned, this was very much in evidence after the London blitz. Rosebay willow-herb was found growing on the bomb-damaged sites. Similarly at Clydebank in Scotland it took up residence at the bombed out site of the Singer sewing machine factory, earning it the name 'Singer-weed'.

The site that the rosebay willow-herb and the willow-herb once occupied was beside the bonfire area in the south east corner of the churchyard.

The plant is noted for its astringency, which is helpful in cases of diarrhoea, and for digestive upsets. This was particularly favoured by the American Eclectic doctors in the 1800s. They used rosebay willow-herb to treat uterine bleeding, and the leaves of the plant for 'foul and indolent ulcers'. Today herbalists might use it to treat Candida overgrowth.

Willow-herb *Epilobium* spp.

Growing nearby this less glamorous plant, but no less useful member of the willow-herb family. It was known and used by the herbalists in days gone by; Culpepper, Gerard and Parkinson. It is astringent and can staunch bleeding. Parkinson made the claims that it could "restrain fluxes, heale the sores of the mouth and secret parts, close up quickly green wounds and heale old ulcers."

Today it is best known to herbalists as a treatment for prostate problems, including benign prostate hyperplasia (BHP). It was the Austrian herbalist Maria Treben who encouraged the use of willow-herb for this purpose. The willow-herb can be combined with pellitory of the wall or couch grass to help women with urinary problems.

Papaveraceae

Poppy *Papaver Rhoeas*

Often known as the 'corn poppy' its bright red colour makes it stand out amongst the yellowing wheat. The petals are very delicate, and prompted the Scottish poet Robert Burns to break into English when he said in his poem Tam O' Shanter.

> "Pleasures are like poppies spread,
> You seize the flower, the bloom is shed."

It is also the flower of Remembrance, having grown on the fields of Flanders, and is now worn by many to think of those lost in battle.

Medicinally the poppy can ease pain. Herbalists might offer it for the easing of asthma, whooping cough and bronchitis. Before the Reformation and the dissolution of the monasteries, the learned monks cared for the sick. They were skilled in the use of plants, growing many for medicinal purposes. Even today around the site of a long-gone monastic establishment, it is possible to find healing plants still growing there. The fictional monk Brother Cadfael was fond of his 'Poppy Juice' which he administered to relieve anxiety and insomnia.

Our native poppy is not as powerful as its cousin, the opium poppy. This is the plant that gives us opium, morphine and heroin. These drugs will alleviate the most severe pain, but must be used with care, as they can become addictive.

The poppy was a rare visitor to the churchyard, but did appear when the ground had been disturbed.

Plantaginaceae – Plantains

Greater plantain *Plantago major*

This is a plant that has survived three ice ages. Its uses go back many centuries to Greek and Roman times. Plantain was regarded as a good treatment for skin conditions, and also to treat syphilis. It is said that Henry VIII found it helpful.

From Europe it was taken by settlers to the colonies as part of their medicine chest. The plant became known as white man's foot as it was found wherever white man settled. Later it became part of the Native American herbal treatments, and was used as an antiseptic, diuretic and general health restorative. Plantain also found its way into the Indian Ayurvedic medical chest. Plantain was used as a plant for snakebites. Early man observed how animals made use of herbs. The French herbalist Maurice Mességué in his book *Of Men and Plants* describes watching a weasel roll in the plantain before attacking a snake. Plantain is also a country cure for nettle stings. On a day to day basis, it was useful for boils, burns, mouth ulcers, sunburn, open sores and much more. This plantain is found throughout the churchyard, and when not flowering the floret of leaves is rather pleasing to look at lying flat amongst the grass.

Ribwort plantain *Plantago lanceolata*

This species has similar qualities to Plantago major, but is better known as a possible treatment for catarrh, sinusitis, glue ear, earache and tinnitus.

The 16th century herbalist John Gerard berated the physicians of the day for searching the world for new cures, when the humble plants like plantain were near at hand and just as effective.

Hoary plantain *Plantago media*

Also known as lamb's tongue

This plantain can be used as a mouthwash, it might relieve toothache, is good for skin problems and can be used as an eyewash. It is said that the seeds used internally can be used as a bulk laxative.

On leaving the church on a summer's evening I spotted two dainty little flowers of the hoary plantain. The light was fading, they looked like two diminutive ballerinas wearing tutus. The light made them look dazzling white, and quite magical. This was one of my memorable discoveries, as I had not met this variety of plantain before.

Over time the plant classifications have changed, new family names have been created, and plants such as the foxglove and speedwell being accepted now as part of the Plantain family.

Foxglove *Digitalis purpurea*

Over the years I believed that there should be foxgloves in the churchyard. Every year I watched and waited for certain leaves on the north side of the church to develop flowers, sadly they didn't make maturity. Then on the 25th June 2016 I couldn't believe my eyes, the most enormous foxglove was standing proud in front of the hedge on the south side, by the ash tree, and opposite the church entrance.

It was taller than the hedge, and had at least sixty bells, being visited by a number of bees. It was monumental. It was the only one.

I visited daily, observing the spent bells at the bottom, whilst further up the new bells were opening, and finally a flourish at the very top. Such a beautiful plant.

As a child I had been warned not to touch the foxgloves at all, they were dangerous, and I should certainly not put my fingers into the bells!

Today we know the foxglove as a heart medicine, but in the herbalist Gerard's day it was not highly regarded: "The Fox-gloves in that they are bitter, are hot and dry, with a certain kind of cleansing quality joined therewith; yet they are of no use, neither have they any place among medicines, according to the Ancients."

Culpeper said this of them, "The leaves have a hot and bitter taste. It is used by the Italians to heal fresh wounds, the leaves being bound thereon. The juice is used to cleanse, dry and heal old sores. The decoction with some sugar or honey cleanses and purges the body both upwards and downwards and opens obstructions of the liver and spleen."

The Celts and Druids did find it useful. The Physicians of Myddfai used the foxglove to regulate the heart beat when taken in small doses, but they recognised in larger doses it would likely be fatal. They were particularly skilled in the use of plants, and indeed were able to perform many surgical procedures using certain plants for anaesthesia.

In fairly recent folk medicine there is a story from Wales of a lady remembering how her mother had eleven children, she breastfed them all, and when the time came to wean them she sent the children into the woods to gather some large leaves of the foxglove, these she put on her breasts like huge plasters, and her milk was dried with no ill effects.

Fashions come and go.

Germander speedwell *Veronica chamaedrys*

Also known as eye of Christ, angel eyes

There is a legend as to how the name Veronica became associated with the speedwell. As Jesus made his way to Calvary, a lady of compassion stepped forward and wiped his brow. One account of the story is that the marks left on Veronica's cloth showed the blue of the little speedwell plant.

Country folk used the speedwell as infusions for quite a number of conditions, as a wound healing plant, coughs, catarrh and skin problems. It was also believed to cure smallpox and measles. It was found throughout the churchyard, and a few years ago there was a proliferation around in the nearby countryside of this stunning blue flower. It may only have been a small flowerhead, but in quantity it certainly it was an arresting sight.

I believe there were other members of the speedwell family in the church yard, but didn't get them documented.

Spring speedwell *Veronica verna*

The gravel path has always had lots of interesting little bits and pieces in it. Last May I spotted the tiniest blue flowers, no more than 2 cm high. They resembled speedwell, and indeed I believe that is what they are. They don't flower for long.

I remember in a summer past noticing the same thing in the grass just at the church gate.

Polygonaceae

Bistort *Persicaria bistorta*

Also known as adderwort, gentle dock, snakeroot

Like many other plants in the churchyard, bistort is used for multiple conditions. It possesses a large amount of tannin. It is the powdered root that would be used and kept for emergencies. A teaspoon in a cup of boiling water could help with all internal bleeding, diarrhoea, dysentery, cholera, as well as haemorrhages from the lungs and stomach.

As the name suggests it could be useful should one be bitten by a snake.

Redshank *Persicaria maculosa*

Also known as arsemart

Culpeper recommends 'Mild Arssmart' for putrid ulcers, worms, toothache, inflammations and green wounds.

Common sorrel *Rumex acetosa*

The culinary herb sorrel is an excellent accompaniment to a fish dish, due to its distinctive lemon flavour.

For many centuries this plant has been revered by noted medicinal herbalists, and amongst those singing its praises are John Parkinson, Nicholas Culpeper, Sir John Hill, John Evelyn and Robert Thornton. A number of claims were made for sorrel, as a prevention against infection, in particular, the plague and scurvy. John Evelyn wrote that "In the making of Sallets (salads), (sorrel) imparts a grateful quickness to the rest as supplying the want of oranges and lemons." It should be noted that in Medieval times and the middle ages folks used a great many different leaves in their salads, stuff we would now call weeds!

Parkinson found this a useful plant, as it could be used instead of lemons, to give a tart flavour to food. This can sharpen the appetite especially in cases when a convalescent requires some encouragement to eat.

It could also alleviate scurvy. Scurvy was so often experienced by sailors who were at sea for great periods of time, when fresh food was unavailable. It was poorly understood that food had an impact on this condition, and so, often after a few days ashore, the sailor's condition improved greatly.

The French explorer Jacques Cartier arrived at Newfoundland in 1534, having lost twenty-five of his men to scurvy. The friendly Huron people cured the rest of the crew with white spruce. It was to take another 200 years for James Lind, the Scottish Royal Navy surgeon to prove that citrus fruit would prevent scurvy; and another 100 years later the Royal Navy decided to give rations of citrus fruit to prevent scurvy. Thereafter men in the navy were given the nickname 'Limeys', which in turn has been said to have helped Britannia to Rule the Waves and create the Commonwealth. Vitamin C was isolated in 1932 and the link to scurvy established.

Even today many of us fail to understand the significance of food and the way it impacts on general health. It may not be scurvy, but cancers, diabetes and heart problems can be improved by diet, maybe not cured, but can go a long way to achieving a better life.

Common garden sorrel was to appear as an early cancer cure. In the 1760s in the USA, the House of Burgesses of the General Assembly of Virginia offered the sum of $100 for the discovery a means to be rid of cancer. It took many years to hear testimonies of supposedly cured patients. The prize winner was herbalist Mrs Mary Johnson. She combined sorrel with greater celandine and persimmon. Dr. Hugh Martin named sorrel a "sovereign specific" for cancer and later cured Caesar Rodney (1728–1784) who went on to be a signatory of the Declaration of Independence.

Sheep's sorrel *Rumex acetosella.*

A very close relative of the Common sorrel is sheep's sorrel. This particular plant was to play a major part in the controversial 'cure' for cancer. Together with burdock, turkey rhubarb and slippery elm it formed a treatment know as Essiac. In the 1920s a Canadian nurse, Rene Caisse came across a cure for cancer. Seemingly she had been given the recipe that had reportedly come from the Ojibwa Indians who were known for their healing powers. Nurse Caisse began treating cancer patients for whom there was no hope. Apparently she amazed many doctors with her treatments and cures, and indeed had a number of doctors as her friends. There is much intrigue in this story. Ralph Moss PhD writer of *Herbs Against Cancer* says that of the four herbs the most likely key ingredient is *Acetosella vulgaris*, or sheep's sorrel. Dr. Charles Brusch, a physician to Senator John Kennedy was known to value sheep's sorrel as a means of treating cancer.

I had been on the hunt for sheep's sorrel for many years, and, finding all sorts of docks and sorrels, but not the one I sought. Fairly recently I had taken a picture of another plant growing against the wall on the south side of the church. Only when I examined the image on my computer did I spot what looked like sheep's sorrel. Returning almost immediately, sure enough, that's what it was. What was so surprising was the size of the leaf, it was so much smaller than I expected it to be. The leaves resembled little fish.

Docks and sorrels rather like growing in the churchyard.

Broad leaf dock *Rumex obtusifolius*

In my earliest years this was my introduction to healing herbs. In those days little children did not have the benefit of protective clothing known as jeans. Therefore, a walk in the woods was bound to end in tears. Nettles lurked everywhere. It was then I was taught to find a dock leaf to rid myself of the pain.

The dock leaf may have been used to treat burns and scalds. They offered a first aid cabinet just outside the homestead in days of old.

It is not just all about the leaves, the root too could be used to make a tea that could cure boils.

A memory of childhood. The seeds of this plant were stripped off, and the orangey pink seeds made pretend cornflakes when playing 'doll's houses'.

Yellow dock *Rumex crispus*

Also known as curled or crisped dock

Yellow dock can be found on waste ground, and in the churchyard, mainly in the border by the lilac bushes.

Yellow dock is used for skin conditions, eczema, psoriasis, ring worm and shingles. In the past it was used for leprosy.

It has astringent properties which will arrest bleeding both internally and externally, and can combat diarrhoea.

The claims made for it as a healing plant are quite extraordinary. Deposits of this plant have been found from the Palaeolithic age. It is still very relevant today, and research is being carried out regarding the claims that have been made for it. In particular yellow dock is said to have the ability to treat cancer, and also prevent cancer. Yellow dock was used in the cancer treatment formulas of Hoxsey and Caisse.

Clustered Dock *Rumex conglomeratus*

Just another dock growing in the hedge row. Sorrels and docks seem to like the conditions in the churchyard.

Primulaceae

Primrose *Primula vulgaris*

The primrose has been used for gout and rheumatism. It is perhaps better known as a sedative for insomnia, and is said to ease nervous headaches.

On the Outer Hebrides it was once part of a cure for 'bad blood'. This condition manifested itself in boils on the legs. The leaves of the primrose were used underside down, until the poison was drained away, and then the topside of the leaf applied to heal the wound.

Cowslip *Primula veris*

Traditionally has been used for insomnia, and that is still true today. It might be combined with passionflower and hops. If anxiety is the problem, cowslip can be used with valerian.

The root is today used by herbalists for bronchitis and whooping cough

Creeping Jenny *Lysimachia nummularia*

Also known as Moneywort.

Creeping Jenny is a bright yellow flower with a trailing habit. This can make it poplar with some gardener's if used as a ground cover plant, and a pest to others who do not wish it in their lawn. The leaves are round and resemble a trail of coins, hence the common name 'moneywort'.

In Irish folklore Creeping Jenny was brought indoors to bring harmony to the household should there be any bad feelings amongst the family. It was a very useful wound herb, good for skin problems, and aches and pains.

Scarlet pimpernel *Anagallis arvensis*

Also known as poor man's weatherglass, red chickweed, shepherd's barometer, adder's eyes

The sensitive petals of the pimpernel close when the sky darkens as rain threatens, and is likely to be open between 9 in the morning till 3 in the afternoon.

Scarlet pimpernel was once used to treat gallstones, liver and lung problems, Conditions of the eyes were treated with scarlet pimpernel and honey by the Greek physicians, and by Gerard and Culpepper.

Country folk used it to remove splinters and thorns from the flesh.

The distilled water or juice of the plant is said by the French to "cleanse the skin from any roughness, deformity or discolourings thereof."

Ranunculaceae

Bulbous buttercup *Ranunculus bulbosus*

This amazing plant is said to be 130 million years old. The buttercup has to be one of the best known of all the countryside wildflowers.

In spite of looking cheery in the meadows, livestock avoid eating it due its toxic nature. The leaves are an irritant and can cause blistering to the mouths of cattle. Most animals have the sense to be wary of eating it.

However, this 'blistering' effect is of use to the herbalist. The following information is from Mrs Grieve's *A Modern Herbal*. The buttercup possesses the property of inflaming and blistering the skin. Bizarre as it seems there are conditions that require this treatment; it is said to be of benefit especially to those suffering painful joints or gout. Blisters on the wrists can relieve rheumatism. Certain severe headaches can be relieved by applying the juice to the nostrils, and the resulting violent sneezing is said to bring about a cure.

Cases of sciatica and shingles are said to respond to a buttercup tincture. The homeopathic preparation of buttercup is used for similar complaints as the herb, rheumatic and neuralgic conditions; skin eruptions, shingles and herpes.

Meadow buttercup *Ranunculus acris*
Creeping buttercup *Ranunculus repens*
Goldilocks buttercup *Ranunculus auricomus*

There are at least four buttercups in the churchyard. They thrive throughout. The last one I found was the Goldilocks.

It was different in style from the others, and was growing on an old tree stump, and looking superior to the others. The name 'Goldilocks' made it sound much more exotic than creeping, bulbous or field!

John Wesley recommended the buttercup as a plaster which would be applied to the head in the case of severe headaches. The resulting blisters were said to bring about relief.

Today it is used by homeopaths for eczema and skin conditions.

Wood anemone *Anemone nemorosa*

Also known as wind-flower

Wind-flower tends to grow in great swathes underneath the trees in the woods. They seem the perfect flower to herald the spring, symbolising innocence and purity. On the other hand, in ancient history the Chinese called it the 'Flower of Death'.

In the days of Culpeper and Gerard this sweet looking but acrid plant was used for headaches, gout and leprosy. It has fallen out of favour, and no longer used.

The Romans preferred to use the flowers as a protection against becoming ill.

I was delighted to find a few of the flowers amongst the old graves.

Lesser celandine *Ficaria verna*

As its Latin name suggests, it is a member of the buttercup family. It looks like a lower growing version, and has a more open flower. Its common name is 'pilewort' and that was how it was known in Culpeper's day, as now. Lesser celandine can be found in herbal creams, and is said to bring about relief from haemorrhoids.

Rosaceae

Dog rose *Rosa canina*

The Greek poet Sappho named the Rose the 'Queen of flowers'. Robert Burns likened his love to a 'red, red rose'. The Romans believed that the petals had aphrodisiac qualities, and would spread them on the bridal bed. Today we might use rose petals as confetti at weddings. It is a flower that speaks of romance.

In the east hedge of the churchyard the dog rose flourishes. The fruit, the rose-hip played a vital part in children's health, preventing winter colds in the form of rose-hip syrup. The hips had another use, not nearly so worthy. The contents of the hips made 'itchy powder'. It seemed a good idea to put it down the back of a garment and watch the victim squirm in class, but not much fun to be on the receiving end.

Blackberry *Rubus fruticosus*

Commonly known as bramble.

For those of us fortunate enough to live in the country or

the outskirts of town, this plant needs no introduction! 'Blackberrying' was often undertaken in groups in the summer holidays, and the fruit turned into puddings and jams. It was an extremely pleasant way to take vitamin C. The effort of the pickers was marked by the cruel scratches to the limbs in the endeavour to collect this bountiful, but hard earned crop.

The blackberry is an opportunist plant, and will quickly and aggressively occupy any piece of waste ground. It is of the Rosaceae family; the flowers in early summer are pink and white, and in autumn the leaves of the arching branches turn into pretty shades of crimson and red. It was said that the berries should be picked before Michaelmas, otherwise the Devil would claim them, and they were not fit to eat thereafter. Indeed it was often regarded as a plant of the Devil because of the evil nature of the thorns.

In the era of magical medicine, passing babies and people through the branching loops of blackberry was thought to cure ruptures, rheumatism and boils. The loops can be quite large and accommodating at times.

It is commonly known that the leaves have astringent properties, and used to stop bleeding, and relieve diarrhoea. During the American Civil War, 1861–65, the 'Tennessee trots' or 'runs' was an unwanted misery, killing twice as many men than those who fell in battle. Truces were called so that the soldiers from both sides could collect blackberry leaves for tea to alleviate this problem.

Blackthorn *Prunus spinosa*

Also known as sloe

The blackthorn flowers in early spring, flowering snow white on the black twigs and branches. It is an arresting sight. Later the green leaves appear, and later still, the sloes. To gather the fruit, one again has to negotiate the protective thorns, and it takes a while to do so. The rewards come later when sipping the sloe gin on the cold winter evenings.

Like the herbalists of old, today's herbalists regard the blackthorn as a complete bowel medicine, the flowers make a gentle laxative while the fruits are binding.

Culpeper used the sloes as an astringent and useful for fluxes and haemorrhages. It makes a useful mouthwash and can tone up the gums to help keep loose teeth.

The flowers can make a purge and can also be used to expel wind.

There are a number of plants that are claimed as The Devil's Plants, usually jaggy and stingy, the previous three are in that category. They all have thorns.

I have always been fascinated by areas in arable fields that have been left, not just uncultivated but positively impenetrable. It was once said that people living off the land would give the Devil a patch of his own, in the hope of ensuring a good crop for themselves. On the other hand, many people say prayers. The Rogation Service is conducted in the farming communities by the Church in order to pray for, and bless the fields in the hope of a good harvest. So between one and the other, was this the origin of hedging one's bets?

Bullace *Prunus domestica*

Beside the blackthorn on the south hedge I noticed another shrubby and rather stunted tree which I assumed was a cherry plum. The flowers of the two were almost identical, indeed I thought they were the same. However it turned out to be bullace.

Mrs Grieve tells us that the bark, root and branches of this plant are 'considerably' styptic. Almost in every way it resembles the blackthorn, but without the thorns.

Wood aven *Geum urbanium*

Also known as blessed herb, herb bennet or St Benedict's herb, clove root

The first name indicates the power that it was deemed to have for warding off evil, in particular the Devil. Printed in 1491, the *Ortus Sanitatis* states, "Where the root is in the house, Satan can do nothing and flies from it, wherefore it is blessed before all other herbs, and if a man carries a root about him no venomous beast can harm him."

A legend that relates to St Benedict tells that a monk offered him a goblet of poisoned wine. When the saint blessed it, the poison being a sort of devil, flew out of glass causing it to shatter, therefore implicating the monk in an act or treachery. In the olden days, plants were known and studied for their deeper meanings, and a plants such as avens having three leaves indicated the Holy Trinity, and the five petals, the wounds of Christ.

The botanical name Geum from the Greek geno, to give

a pleasant clove-like fragrance. This comes from the roots when dug up. Physicians of old recommended that the root should be dug up on the 25th March (as the soil should be dry by then), this was when the root was said to be most fragrant. The housewife might use the sliced root to scent her bedlinen, and prevent moths, as well as being used to give flavour to her ale.

It was also used as a breath freshener, and worn as an amulet against evil, also the root was believed to have astringent, styptic and febrifuge qualities.

Culpepper used it for "diseases of the chest or breath, for pains and stitches in the sides, it dissolveth inward congealed blood occasioned by falls and bruises, and the spitting of blood… it is a good preservative against the plague or any other poison, It is very safe and is fit to be kept in every body's house."

It was regarded as good for the heart and liver. Cosmetically is might have been used as a washing solution to remove spots and marks on the skin.

Today it would still be used in cases of diarrhoea, dysenteries, fevers, haemorrhages and headache.

… I am so grateful to have a modern computer, spelling is not my strong point, and without a spell-check I would be sunk. The computer does though have an annoying habit of changing what I write, to what it thinks I mean, hence Geum urbanum became Grumpy urbanism!

Barren strawberry *Potentilla sterilise*

The leaves of this tiny plant are said to help with urinary tract Infections; used as a gargle for sore throats; as a diuretic, and may help check diarrhoea.

The fruits are a source of vitamin C and iron and can be used to alleviate anaemia. The Swedish botanist Linnaeus claimed that he cured his gout by eating strawberries. Found amongst the old graves.

Silverweed *Potentilla anserina*

Commonly known as Prince's feathers

This handsome low growing plant does indeed have a silvery appearance to the leaves which resemble a feather, hence also known as Prince's feathers. The flower is bright yellow and attractive to bees. To country folk of old a strong infusion of it was used to check diarrhoea.

As a treatment for cramp, a compress of infused silverweed is reputed to help when applied to the affected areas.

William Salmon, medical practitioner of the Restoration era in London (1710), had this to say of the virtues of silverweed,

> It is very cold and dry in the second degree, astringent, anodyne, vulnerary and arthritic. It stops all fluxes of the bowels, even the bloody flux, also spitting, vomiting of blood, or any inward bleeding. It helps the whites in women and is profitable against ruptures in children and is good to dissipate contusions, fastens loose teeth and heals wounds or ulcers in the mouth, throat or in

any part of the body, drying up old, moist, corrupt and running sores. It resists the fits of agues, is said to break the stone, and is good to cool inflammation in the eyes, as eke to take away all discolourings of the skin and to cleanse it from any kind of depredation.

His predecessor Culpeper held much the same opinion of the plant.

In many cultures silverweed has been used as a food crop. It was found in the lower grassy part of the churchyard at the east end.

Tormentil *Potentilla erecta*

Also known as bloodroot, ewe daisy, English sarsaparilla

This is a delicate looking plant, found at the east end of the churchyard. It has four beautiful shaped petals, unlike the silverweed and cinquefoil with five.

Culpeper said of tormentil, "The root taken inwardly is most efficacious to help any flux in the belly, stomach, spleen or blood. The juice opens obstructions of the liver and lungs, and thereby helps the jaundice."

In those far off days it was also considered useful for wounds, sores, mouth ulcers and general 'hurts'. In many parts of the country, for example in the Highlands and Islands of Scotland the 'herb-wives' used tormentil to treat diarrhoea and dysentery. The active ingredient was tannin.

The tannin content had another very important use, the ability to tan leather. Leather was usually treated with the tannin from the oak, but in areas without trees there had to be another solution.

William Maple produced a leaflet in the early 1700s *A Method of Tanning Without Bark*, stating that the roots of the tormentil could be used successfully instead. A shortage of trees in the Faroes, Ireland and Scottish Islands resorted in a huge demand for the rhizomes of the tormentil, for just such a process.

Cinquefoil *Potentilla reptans*

Cinquefoil is also known as five fingers and five-finger blossom. The yellow flower resembles the buttercup.

Tannins give cinquefoil its astringency, which makes it a useful plant for washing wounds, and it can staunch bleeding.

According to Culpeper, this action is useful internally within the mouth, and can relieve the pain of toothache. It is also used as a gargle for sore mouths and quinsy. Taken with honey cinquefoil can ease hoarseness and act as a cough medicine. There is an impressive list of ailments that can be cured, jaundice, ulcers, cancers, fistulas, running sores, ruptures and to stop internal bleeding and bruising. Culpeper also claims that cinquefoil can reduce a fever, treat inflammation, cure falling sickness, treat gout and sciatica. Almost a 'cure-all'!

David Conway in his book *The Magic of Herbs* states that cinquefoil was a favourite nerve herb of the gipsies. They used it as powerful sedative in cases of hysteria, epilepsy and schizophrenia.

Today it is still used as a gargle for sore throats, and stopping diarrhoea.

Cinquefoil has been used medicinally since the time of the Greek physicians Hippocrates, circa 460–377 BC, and after him Dioscorides circa AD 40–90. It is likely that the usage would go considerably further back, as most herbs would have had an oral tradition.

Agrimony *Agrimonia eupatoria*

Also known as church steeples, sticklewort, cockleburr

Agrimony does indeed resemble church steeples. It is a really attractive plant, found near the hedge at the south east end of the graveyard.

Agrimony is a corruption of the Greek argemon, meaning a white speck on the cornea of the eye; and in those days the 'argemone' was said to bring relief to those suffering eye problems, and used in the treatment of cataracts.

It was a famous wound healer, and was an ingredient of *eau de arquebusade,* which was used particularly to treat musket wounds, as suggested by the term arquebus, which was the 15th century word for musket.

Agrimony is one of the special 57 plants used by the Anglo Saxons. A Holy Salve of this plant was reputed to protect humans from goblins!

At a later period, monks grew Agrimony and used it as a cure for stomach pains, and a compress for open wounds. Culpeper used agrimony with old swine's grease to apply on sores, ulcers and cancers. He recommended it for the removal of thorns and splinters of wood that had become embedded in the flesh.

The 16th century herbalist Gerard prescribed agrimony for 'naughty livers' and Culpeper too believed that agrimony was useful for the liver and jaundice. In folk medicine the colour of the plant often denoted the area of the body that would benefit from the plant, yellow did apply to livers.

A careful study of agrimony showed that it does indeed possess antioxidant and liver protective properties. Agrimony is used as an herb, as a Bach Flower Remedy, and in homeopathy. It is a surprisingly useful plant.

As a footnote, a spray of agrimony was placed under the pillow of our Medieval ancestors to ensure a good night's sleep!

Meadowsweet *Spiraeae latifola Filipendula ulmaria*

Meadowsweet a beautiful summer flower has been used by the ancients, to ease pain, bring down fevers and to soothe the stomach. It can be found growing in the shady area of the hedge to the east of the church.

It has a pleasing fragrance and at one time was used as a strewing herb. The herbal uses of the plant were no greater than many other plants to treat similar conditions, but in the fullness of time, its Latin name would bring it great fame, it would go down in history as the first modern drug. The full story is in Part Two.

Hawthorn *Cratagus oxycantha*

Hawthorn hedges – 'haw' is the old name for hedge, have been a feature of our landscape for at least 8,000 years. Hawthorn contributes much to our folk lore, both Pagan and Christian. Once upon a time the leaves were eaten by our forefathers. They were thought to be sustaining, and known as 'bread and cheese'.

This is a healing plant, and for many centuries country folk would seek out a spring with hawthorn growing beside it; there the pilgrims would leave a piece of cloth tied to the tree, thus looking for a cure for their ailments. It is still possible to find hawthorn used in this way in remote and secret parts of the country.

The red berries of the hawthorn are particularly healing, and used by the learned Druids as a heart medicine, who also used foxglove for the heart. However, by the time Culpepper, Gerard and Parkinson were practicing in the 17th century, the hawthorn was used for 'the (kidney) stone', removal of splinters and for diarrhoea. No mention of the heart! At that time the foxglove too was of no value. "Neither have they any place in medicines," said Gerard.

Both plants treat the heart, the hawthorn is much milder than the foxglove. Both have their basis in Druid medicine.

Modern science does indeed prove the usefulness of hawthorn for those suffering from heart disease.

Rubiaceae

Lady's bedstraw *Galium verum*

A field of lady's bedstraw is a wonderful sight to behold. As if it is not enough to have a feast for the eyes, the scent was absolutely beautiful, and so memorable. In the churchyard there was a small amount around the old graves immediately by the east wall. Legend has it that this plant lined the manger where Jesus lay.

Parkinson recommends this plant for urinary tract infections, although that was not what they were called back then. It has styptic qualities, for nose bleeds, and as a component of an ointment to soothe burns and scalds. Weary travellers carried lady's bedstraw to help them on their way.

Used externally, lady's bedstraw can be used for skin disorders, psoriasis, blackheads and wounds.

All these plants are strewing herbs, as used in olden days. They possess red dye, the Native Americans used these plants to dye feathers.

Hedge bedstraw *Galium album*

This has white flowers and in the churchyard, as the name suggests, uses the hedges for support. It is similar to the lady's bedstraw in that they can both be used to treat bladder and kidney stones, and clear the body of toxic waste.

Both plants are strewing herbs, as used in olden days.

Upright bedstraw *Galium subsp*

There was only one bit of it, standing upright amongst the old graves. As the Latin name suggests, it is a subspecies of the hedge bedstraw. One presumes that it could treat the same conditions as the above.

Cleavers *Galium aparine*

From the word cleave, meaning to stick. Also known as sticky willie, goose grass, sweethearts.

Our ancestors had a number of practical uses for the plant. After milking, the frothy white liquid harboured many 'foreign bodies' therefore a strainer was required. A ball of cleavers was just the thing to remove any nasties from the milk.

Cleavers made an excellent vegetable, the leaves could be eaten like spinach, and the seeds roasted to make a coffee substitute.

In the past many children would take harmless pleasure out of attaching a piece of this sticky plant to the back of a victim. Innocent fun. The purpose of the adherent characteristic of the plant was nature's way of dispersing the seeds; humans and animals help in this procedure. Today herbalists might use this plant as a lymphatic tonic, a diuretic, as a means of relieving urinary infections, and to help the lowering of the blood pressure.

Woodruff *Galium odoratum*

Woodruff colonised the whole churchyard. It popped up everywhere and seemed like a filler if there were any spaces left to fill. Woodruff was regarded as a good treatment for the liver and spleen. Culpeper used an interesting phrase, "it is said to be a proactive to venery." That quite simply is sexual love. I wonder how many people knew that in the olden days? Today an herbalist might use it to treat insomnia.

Field madder *Sherardia arvensis*

About a mile away from the church I had spotted what looked like thyme. The colours were about right, and the flower was tiny. On a sunny May evening I found the same plant within a corner of the two flint walls of the church. On a closer inspection I noted that the flower formed a little cross, it was a member of the crosswort family, but not thyme ! Being unknown to me I decided that it might be squinancy wort, a specific for the treatment of quinsy, a pretty serious throat problem that nowadays requires treatment in hospital. It wasn't that.

So, back to the drawing board. My friends thought it might be field madder, and this is what it proved to be. It grows on arable land. Sadly, it has no known medicinal qualities, but worth mentioning anyway, and it produces a dye.

Scrophulariaceae

Dark mullein *Verbascum nigra*

Mullein is an eye-catching plant, and doesn't go unnoticed. It has been of use to man for some considerable time. In Culpeper's day, mullein was a useful treatment for coughs and spitting blood. More recently it could be used with coltsfoot and other herbs used for disorders of the lungs.

Mullein was smoked from the earliest times, long before nicotine arrived on our shores. The smoke aided breathing, and on a summer evening might have kept the flies away.

An oil can be made from it which is helpful in cases of severe earache. It is often used in conjunction with garlic oil, the mullein oil going into the ear first, then the garlic, as the garlic would be likely to burn the sensitive inner ear.

With regards to the day-to-day uses, a leaf might be used as an insole for the weary traveller, it might make the walk just a little bit easier. It is astonishing to think that not so many years ago, the only way the poor could get from A to B was on foot. Today we think of enjoying a stroll on the country lanes on a sunny day, but that could never have been the case then. We might have a small ruck sack with some water or coffee, but the travellers would have been shouldering the load, in all weathers.

The tall stem acted as a wick when used with animal fat, therefore bringing light into the home.

Solanaceae

Bittersweet *Solanum dulcamara*

Also known as woody nightshade, felonwort

Bittersweet is a close relative of the tomato, the flowers are very similar. Bittersweet has pretty purple petals and bright yellow stamens. The flowers hang in clusters, just like the tiny sweet tomatoes. Bittersweet has the ability to climb in a vine like fashion, and after the flowers and leaves have gone, the bright red berries continue to decorate the hedgerows into early winter.

The generic name Solanum comes from *solor* which means 'I ease', suggesting a medicinal use for the plant. The name 'bittersweet' is said to come from the Middle Ages when a piece of root might be chewed, and it was found to initially taste bitter, and then develop sweetness. This is not something to be recommended today. The berries in particular are likely to cause vomiting.

Bittersweet is of the nightshade family and considered poisonous.

Before the arrival of antibiotics, country folk suffering whitlows may have used the crushed berries to alleviate the pain. Bittersweet's common name felonwort, is another name for whitlow. Bittersweet is narcotic and can rid the body of impurities, therefore it may in fact have had some value in the treatment of whitlows.

Gerard says of it: "The juice is good for those that have fallen from high places, and have been thereby bruised or beaten, for it is thought to dissolve blood congealed or cluttered anywhere in the intrals and to heale the hurt places."

In the past it was used for skin complaints, psoriasis, eczema, and skin diseases; also rheumatism, kidney problems, bronchitis, jaundice, asthma and syphilis. In fact until 1907 it was included in the British Pharmacopoeia.

Culpepper suggested that a garland could be hung around the neck to cure vertigo, while farmers and shepherds might have used it as charms around the necks of cattle and sheep to protect against the evil eye.

Homeopaths prepare it today for chronic bronchial catarrh, asthma and whooping cough.

Black nightshade *Solanum nigrum*

This is an annual herb, about half a metre tall, it has oval leaves with small whitish violet flowers, with fruit being green to start with turning purplish black. It was also found in the south hedge, not far from the bittersweet.

In the right hands this is a very useful plant, but like all the nightshade family, it is poisonous, and needs to be used with great care. An herbalist of old would have used it to bring down a fever, to purge, to kill pain and to sedate.

Urticaceae

Nettle *Urtica dioica*

The nettle is probably the most recognisable plant as it stings the unwary, and the pain is sufficient to pose a warning to watch out for it! In spite of this, it is a remarkable plant. It has survived a number of ice ages. To flourish, the Nettle needs fertile soil, moisture and sunlight. Early man cleared forests, thereby giving it a chance to flourish. To our ancestors the nettle had many uses. It was the first green to appear in the spring, and was a most welcome supplement to the diet. In Sweden it is grown as a farm crop, as hay for animals and it is said can increase milk production in cows. In Scotland the fibrous stalks were treated in the same way as flax to make bed linen and tablecloths. During the First World War the Germans made soldiers uniforms from the nettle. Green plant dye is obtained from the leaves, and yellow from the roots. As a medical plant, much research is being carried out to the claims that have been made as to the efficacy of the remedies.

There is an impressive list of ailments that can be remedied by the nettle, whether used as a tea, tincture or poultice.

Allergies – hay fever, antihistamine

Arthritic conditions – anti-inflammatory, arthritis, gout, osteoporosis pain, rheumatism, sciatica

Circulatory – anaemia, astringent, blood cleanser (spring tonic), haemorrhoids, internal bleeding, nose bleeds, uterine haemorrhage

Digestive Tract – constipation, diarrhoea, dysentery, gingivitis

Hormonal Problems – lactation, excessive menstruation, hot flushes, PMS

Immune System – anti- histamine, immune booster, lupus erythematosus, multiple sclerosis

Mental – Alzheimer's

Prostate – enlarged prostate

Respiratory – asthma, bronchitis, tuberculosis

Skin and Hair -boils and spots, eczema, childhood and nervous dandruff, lacklustre hair, premature balding in men, prickly heat

Urinary – bladder infections, diuretic

Weight loss

Notable sponsors of the use of nettle such as Dr Christopher, Dr James Duke and the preacher John Wesley have raised the virtue of the plant for all things to do with joints, arthritis, gout and rheumatism. Modern science supports this in that the plant contains boron which aids healthy bones. The plant will also eliminate the uric acid that so often causes the problem.

Scientific studies in Germany confirm the beneficial effect on the enlarged prostate gland, and the combination of the nettle roots with saw palmetto was found to be equal to the prescription drug for the same purpose, but without the side effects.

The presence of boron in nettles is proving useful in cases of Alzheimer's in improving short-term memory.

According to Dr Duke, there is a form of therapy for MS sufferers which involves being stung by bees. He suggests a similar treatment, the self-flailing with the nettle. He recommends keeping a potted one for this purpose, so is at hand, with something to hold on to! He has two reasons for nettle preference, the bee will die after this treatment, whilst the nettle will recover, and also bee stings can often cause severe allergic reactions in some people, and in some cases death might result from the bee sting.

If one wishes to collect this plant to eat as salad, or make soup with it should be done before mid-summer as the leaves turn bitter at that point. It can also be hung in shady place to dry for tea. I did once sample the leaves in salad, they had first been treated and rolled in olive oil, and did not sting the mouth; not something I've been brave enough to try it at home!

In the later months of the year this nettle looks extremely menacing. It is a tall plant, and displays a full show of seed pods, dark and greyish green in colour. Seen swaying in the wind, it really suggests it is not a plant to be meddled with.

"This stunningly useful herb is ridiculously underused" A. Vogel Institute.

Nettle small *Utrica urens*

Urtica urens is a smaller version of the dioica.

The small nettle is used in much the same way as the large, for gout, rheumatism, lactation and allergies. It is more usual to find the small nettle prepared and presented as homeopathy.

Of the nettle plants there is a belief that they were introduced to Britain at the time of the Roman invasion. It was understood that the men from warmer climates found it difficult to deal with the cold and damp. They were said to flog themselves with the nettles to keep warm.

Some fifteen years ago the following appeared in a column written in the *Telegraph* by Dr James le Fanu, "Readers may recall the saga of the Hebridean grandmother much afflicted by arthritis who had found that the most effective treatment was – irrespective of the weather – to strip off completely and 'roll naked in a bed of nettles'."

This treatment is not unknown to many older people suffering this condition. Perhaps one day the active ingredients can be bottled and used in the comfort of one's home.

Both nettles thrive under the hedges around the churchyard

Even as a child I heard mention of nettles being a spring tonic after all the heavy winter food, it was thought of as a blood purifier, and a means of treating acne.

Pellitory of the Wall *Parietaria judaica*

Pellitory makes itself at home close to walls. The Latin for wall is paries, so both English and Latin names detail exactly where it grows. Pellitory has dark green leaves, and reddish stalks with tiny pink flowers, and it can grow two feet tall. I found this plant on the south side of the church growing on the flint wall. This was the first one I had come across, and it took time to identify it. The soil was poor against the wall, but it thrived.

In Europe, pellitory is used to treat herpes zoster (shingles). This has led to the investigative research that might offer treatment for other viral infections. One such piece of research is into treatment for FIV, a form of HIV that attacks cats.

Pellitory has been known to cause asthma, so best avoided by those who suffer allergies.

Violaceae

Violet Dog *Viola riviniana*

Violets have had a long history of being used to heal skin malignancies. One of the first to champion this theory was Saint Hildegard of Bingen (1098-1179). Her ideas on cures came, she said, from God. "In all creation, trees, plants, animals and gem stones, there are hidden secret powers which no person can know unless they are revealed by God." Recently her cancer salve has been studied and found to contain violets.

Violets have been used in Russian folk medicine, for the treatment for cancerous sores. At the moment trials are ongoing as to the possibilities of using the violet as a template for a new medicinal treatment of skin cancer. On a recent trip to the Cambridge Botanical Gardens the floral feature 'Healthy Herbie' had information boards with the attributes of the plants displayed. On the board relating to Skin Cancers (Carcinoma) it stated that common figwort and violet may be useful models for drugs in the future.

Maurice Mességué used violet sweets to help with irritable coughs. In his book he mentions giving them to Sir Winston Churchill.

Mosses, lichen, ferns and fungi

Mosses *Sphagnum cymbifolium, papillose, palustre*

I only realised they were there when I had nothing else to write about. I spotted them at the beginning of 2014, and remembered the significance of moss in the WWI war effort to supply dressings to the front. This is written about in Part Two.

Mosses are fascinating things, and warrant a study all of their own. When as a Girl Guide camping in a most beautiful setting outside Edinburgh, I had a chance to view mosses close up. One afternoon for the rest hour I wandered into the woods. There were shafts of sunshine lighting up patches of moss. Upon lying down to get a closer look, found myself amazed by the variety of different mosses. It was quite magical.

Lichens *Caloplaca flavenscens*

I suddenly spotted the lichens, on the stones, the flints and the trees! My photographs on the computer gave me a chance to fully appreciate the growths. They were quite beautiful, but perhaps wise not be embarking on yet another study, otherwise this book will never get finished!

Ferns

Hart's tongue fern *Phyllitis scolopendrium Asplenium scolopendrium*

This simple fern grows in the cracks of walls or rocks, in a shady position. In Culpeper's time this fern was used for liver and spleen problems, hiccoughs, passions of the heart, and bleeding gums. Today it is used as a liver tonic; diuretic and for bronchial disease.

Wall rue *Asplenium Ruta-muraria*

Also known as white maidenhair, tentwort

This tiny little plant, 2–3 inches high was nearly missed as it was growing snugly in the flint on the north side of the church. It grew in a small bunch. I could not have guessed that it was classed as a fern. The shade of green is similar to the herb rue. In spite of not being related the two plants have similar properties.

It was once used for children's conditions; a condition known as 'tentwort' better known a rickets. Wall rue was said to have been a specific cure. Also useful for children's coughs and ruptures. This was surprise find.

Lady fern *Athyrium filix-femina*

Ferns are reputed to be used for ridding the body of worms, a vermifuge. The most powerful of these is the male fern. Oil extracted from the male fern was a vital ingredient since the times of Dioscorides. However, in more primitive times a fern was a fern, and one used what was at hand. The churchyard fern joined the two above on the damp flint wall.

Fungi

Psilocybin *Psilocybe semilanceata*

On a few occasions I have come across some fungi, and just snapped them. Not something I know anything about, so there was never an intention to write about them.

I was then told that they were of huge interest to the scientific community at present with regards finding uses for them that help with all manner of mental and emotional conditions. How could I not wish to find out more?

Puffball *Lycoperdon perlatum*

This was certainly my oddest find in the churchyard, found in the old graves.

As to its medicinal uses, it could be used to treat Candida albicans according to *Potter's Herbal*.

Puffballs have been found in the Neolithic settlement in Orkney. They may have been used as a wound dressing; the inside of the Puffball is astringent, thus arresting bleeding.

Trees

Aceraceae

Field maple *Acer campestre*

This graceful tree grows in the hedge beside the hazel on the east side. Maples are known for their syrupy secretions, which may be collected by tapping.

Culpeper made use of the decoction of the leaves and bark for obstructions of the liver. Today by using the same process, the bark might be used for sore eyes.

Of the tree itself, it produces valued wood, which is a favourite of cabinet makers

The grain of the wood is compact, and often used for vegetable chopping boards as the wood appears to self repair after cutting.

Sycamore *Acer pseudoplatanus*

Culpeper extols the virtue of the sycamore thus:

> The Juice, or milk is taken from the tree by piercing the bark, and dried. It is then made into troches and applied to tumours which it softens and dissolves. It also solders together the lips of fresh wounds. The fruit can be applied as a plaster to achieve the same effect.

The word 'troche' was new to me, the best description I could find was 'lozenge'.

Sycamore is not in use at the present time, but one never knows when it might be of interest to researchers in the future.

Aquifoliaceae

Holly *Ilex aquifolium*

> *"The Holly and the Ivy*
> *When they are both full grown*
> *of all the trees that are in the wood*
> *The Holly wears the crown*
> *The rising of the sun*
> *And the running of the deer*
> *The playing of the merry organ*
> *Sweet singing in the choir."*

The above is one of today's most loved Christmas carols Its roots go back to pre-Christian times when holly and ivy were taken indoors for the midwinter period. The shiny dark green leaves and the red berries are still very much the colours associated with Christmas.

Holly was once used as a treatment for many winter ailments, but these remedies are no longer in fashion. The berries are regarded as poisonous.

Betulaceae

Hazel *Corylus avellana*

The hazel is one of the our most ancient trees, and in the churchyard of St. Mary's it grows by the eastern hedge alongside our other indigenous trees, the ash, field maple, hawthorn, holly and elder with the oak growing by the church boundary. It grows to about ten metres tall. As with most trees, the flowers appear before the leaves as catkins, known by country folk as lamb's tails. When the nursery rhyme 'Little Bo Peep' is illustrated, it often shows the hazel sporting the 'lamb's tails'.

This tree was revered for its magic and mysticism. Our ancient ancestors sensed those powers. It is said that the tree possesses quick moving and mercurial energies, like that of the silver-fish and snakes. The hazel is associated to the God Mercury, he travels through the air, with winged hat and sandals, and carrying the staff of hazel. This staff is seen adorned with ribbons, which entwine themselves around the staff, in a manner similar to the silver snakes. It is this staff that is the symbol of physicians today.

The hazel was of great use to our ancestors, the branches are extremely pliable, therefore suitable for making coracles, fishing rods, springels (like giant hair-grips) to hold thatch in place, bean poles, wattles, for basket making and hoops. Also to make beaters to flush pheasants and game-birds from their cover. A carefully cut fork of hazel in the hands of a dowser will move to indicate the presence of underground water, an essential when sinking wells. Early on it was discovered that the wood could be made into charcoal which, when burned gave off a greater heat than wood alone. Roger Bacon discovered that hazel charcoal together with saltpetre and sulphur made gunpowder.

Druids and Celts observed hazel growing by a pool shedding its nuts, then eaten by the salmon, a wise and magical fish. The ancients understood long before it could be proven scientifically that salmon could find their way back to the pool where they were spawned.

When used as cure, Culpepper advised powdering the dried husks and shells, taken in red wine to "stay the laxness of the bowel and women's courses." An old cough was treated with the kernels in mead or honeyed water; and if pepper was added it might draw the rheum from the head.

According to recent medical studies it seems that the leaves have a number of properties that might heal wounds and cleanse the body of toxins. They have been used to treat ulcers, varicose veins, rashes and infections.

Finally, to think of the hazelnut is to be reminded of the writings of Julian of Norwich:

> In this vision he showed me a little thing, the size of a hazelnut, and it was round as a ball. I looked at it with the eye of my understanding and thought "What may this be?" And it was generally answered thus: "It is all that is made." I marvelled how it might last, for it seemed it might suddenly have sunk into nothing because of its littleness. And I was answered in my understanding: "It lasts and ever shall, because God loves it."

Fagaceae

Oak *Quercus roubo*

The very name 'oak' suggests might and strength. For centuries the oak has been used as a building material, used in many great buildings requiring roof vaults, and used as wood of choice from the early ships, especially war ships as used to face the Spanish Armada.

The oak is associated with the magic of midsummer, the oak is king. The roots of the tree are said to be the passage way to the underworld, and only known to the fairies.

The main medicinal property of the oak is the tannin contained in the bark. This is an astringent. A twig from the tree frayed at the end acted as a tooth brush to the ancients. If there was any bleeding from the gum, the astringent would stop it.

Rasputin is thought to have used the astringent properties of the oak to stop the bleeding of the haemophiliac Russian prince, Alexei Romanov, son of Tsar Nicholas II. It may well have done.

When one thinks of the Druids, mistletoe boughs come to mind, and being harvested with a gold sickle. This was used in medicine but became unpopular by the Middle Ages. According to Angela Paine, Rudolph Steiner believed that the Druids of Britain had the answers to healing. In the 1920s he made the journey to Shropshire, England to investigate the mistletoe. There he had a vision, he tuned into the wisdom of the Druids, the mistletoe in Steiner's mind was the cure for cancer. The Oak was the host tree.

Holm oak *Quercus ilex ballota*

John Gerard has little good to say of the holm oak, but it does have a few useful qualities. The galls that form on this tree are very astringent, and like the oak can be used to arrest bleeding, and can cause diarrhoea and dysentery to cease. To a lesser extent, the bark is astringent too.

Oleaceae

Ash *Fraxinus excelsior*

The ash tree is one of our venerated native trees, and today there is great concern about 'ash die back' that is affecting them. Similarly the Dutch elm disease of the 1960s is remembered for robbing the countryside of that other cherished tree. Ash is easily recognised by the hanging bunches of winged seeds commonly known as 'keys'. This tree is made popular in song and verse; 'The Ash Grove', being the best known, and also the song of a young woman traveling far from home and remembering, "O the Oak and the Ash and the bonnie Ivy Tree, They flourish at home in my own country."

When it comes to fires, the ash logs are regarded as the best for burning, as celebrated in the following lines from two versions of the poem 'Logs to Burn'.

> "But Ash-wood green and Ash-wood brown,
> are fit for a queen with a golden crown,
> "But Ash-wood wet and Ash-wood dry,
> a king may warm his slippers by."
> or
> "But Ash logs all smooth and grey,
> burn them green or old,
> Buy up all that come your way,
> they're worth their weight in gold."

> – Honor Goodhart, 1926

The poems were written in 1926 during the miner's strike to inform the housewife what to choose to replace coal. At Christmas time, the Yule log was traditionally the ash, and cut large enough to burn throughout the festive season. The ashes left from the burnt ash logs can be applied as potash to the garden, to enrich the soil, giving nutrients to the crops.

The Ash Tree features in the popular Weather Lore; the old saying that:

> "Oak before Ash, in for a splash,
> Ash before Oak, in for a soak."

In the early times the ash (like many other indigenous trees) seemed to have magical powers to restore good health. The ash symbolised rebirth and new life, so was deemed particularly helpful to babies and small children. To cure a child of rickets, ruptures, hernias and other problems, a young ash tree whilst still growing was split wide enough to pass the suffering child through. This was accompanied by ritual and prayers. The tree was then bound together again, and if the tree survived then so should the child. In the 1788 writings of the Rev. Gilbert White of Selborne, Hampshire, tells of seeing rows of pollarded ashes with seams down the sides, which showed evidence of this practice!

Being such an ancient tree, many healing claims are made for it, and a number of treatments are now being scientifically proven. Mrs. Grieve in her *Modern Herbal* tells that the ash bark, particularly from the roots, has astringent properties. It could be used as a bitter tonic to aid digestion. It is used as an anti-periodic, which means that it could prevent the return of a disease like malaria, which can recur, therefore it acts in much the same way as cinchona, also known as Peruvian bark.

Herbalist Thomas Bartram says that the ash leaf tea is reputed to alleviate gout, rheumatism and sluggish kidney function. It can also be used as a mild laxative. The keys were used by the physicians of old to cure flatulence.

Lilac *Syringa vulgaris*

Lilacs are glorious in the spring, wonderfully scented too. Once upon a time lilac was used in England. It was known as a febrifuge to reduce fevers, and vermifuge to rid the body of worms in the intestines.

It is still used in other parts of the world, Russia being one of them. Lilac has been mentioned in regard of fevers and worms, and also for kidney problems.

Russian Folk Medicine by Paul M Kourennoff (trans. George St George) confirms that the leaves of the lilac were "considered to be a powerful medicinal agent against malaria in all forms." The leaves were used in teas or made into a tincture using alcohol.

Pinaceae

Atlantic cedar *Cedrus atlantica*

This rather magnificent tree rather stands out due to its silvery colour, and is needle-bearing. It is not an indigenous tree, but grown for its ornamentation.

Besides being beautiful, it does have medicinal uses as an aromatherapy oil.

Taxaceae

Yew *Taxus baccata*

The yew is the tree most often associated with the country church. It is a prehistoric tree, and many are thousands of years old. It is thought that the early Christian missionaries preached beneath its canopy, before churches were built.

The yew wood was used for the long bows, and in the 15th century archery practice was compulsory at churches on Sunday afternoons. One had to be ready for invasions those days. The wood of the yew was reckoned to be as hard as iron, and used for ship's masts. Within the churchyard it had many associations with the continuance of life, and once was brought into church at Easter time to symbolise this.

It is used in homoeopathy for skin infections with blisters. A more recent discovery is that of the substance TAXOL, known to many in the last forty years as being the medical treatment for a number of cancers. It is a phyto-medicine, therefore it uses the clippings of the yew hedges to produce the treatment.

Tiliaceae

Lime *Tilia x europaea*

The lime tree is sought out by Scouts and Guides when needing a tool to use for cooking sausages and marshmallows over the camp fire. The twigs are flexible, and less likely to catch a light than many other twigs around.

At the height of summer the honey-scented tree attracts thousands of bees to its flowers, so that one can almost find it from the humming sound alone. There is a bench just below the trees, wonderful to sit in the sunshine to enjoy the sweet scent and listen to the soporific buzzing of the bees.

The flowers are used by the French to make an after-dinner beverage. A perfect way to end a dinner. French herbalist Maurice Mességué describes how his father would put the flowers of the lime into the bath of a fractious child. This created a golden liquid. It ensured a settled and good night's sleep (for everyone)!

Herbalists use lime flowers to treat high blood pressure related to stress, or combined with flowers of the hawthorn to lower blood pressure.

Ulmaceae

Elm *Ulmus procera*

The statuesque English elm was a much loved and fondly remembered tree. It graced the British countryside before succumbing to the Dutch elm disease about 50 years ago.

In Culpeper's time there were many grand claims made for the efficacy of the elm, *Ulmus minor*. He suggested using the leaves and bark with vinegar as a cure for scurf and leprosy. Should you have broken bones, then a bath using a decoction of the leaves, bark and roots should mend them. It could also be used on hard tumours. Not all these sentiments are shared by modern herbalists; today for instance they might use the slightly astringent decoction as a treatment for skin diseases such as ringworm. A homeopathic preparation can be made to treat skin eruptions and ulcerated conditions. For winter colds, sore throats and bronchitis the bark was chewed to bring about relief.

By far the most common of the elm preparations is from the American elm, known as slippery elm. It is similar to the common elm, but much more effective. A powder is produced from the bark, and this unappetising looking substance is then made into a thin paste using milk. It can be used as a nourishing invalid food. Slippery elm also has the ability to soothe the whole of the alimentary canal, treating indigestion, reflux, diarrhoea, constipation, irritable bowel syndrome and inflammatory bowel disease. In cases of dysentery or diarrhoea where other treatments have failed, slippery elm liquid can be injected into the bowel.

In days gone by the wood from the elm tree was valued for its closeness of grain, unlikely to split, and free from knots. It also was able to withstand being wet, therefore used in boat building, and used for water pipes. Elm went into the building of sheds, wagons, carts and furniture.

It is not recommended as a firewood, and according to the old rhyme;

> *"Elm wood burns like churchyard mould,*
> *E'en the very flames are cold."*

The elm is linked to death and the underworld. To the Celts, the elm trees were special to the elves, who guarded the burial mounds.

The Greek hero Orpheus used the music of his harp to enchant those preventing him from rescuing Eurydice.

Once she was free, he played his harp, and it is said that the first elm grove appeared.

Wych elm *Ulmus glabra*

The inner bark of the wych elm has also been used in traditional medicine as a remedy for rheumatism, when used internally as a tisane or externally on the affected area. It has astringent properties and is said to be a useful remedy for diarrhoea. The tisane made from this also has a mildly diuretic action. This small seedling arrived by itself, and took root between two stones in the old section of the churchyard. It grew quickly, every year becoming more established. Recently it had to be cut down, it was quite surprising to see just how large the circumference of the trunk had become in a relatively short time.

The Relationship between Man and Trees

Centuries ago, the lands in the northern hemisphere were heavily wooded. Man was nomadic. When they did settle they cleared the trees to allow for planting crops and to create grazing for their domesticated animals. The felled wood provided shelter, and offered a means cooking and keeping warm. Simple tools could be fashioned from the wood, in in time man knew which tree supplied the best wood for roofs, wheels, cart shafts, etc.

Within the clearings, plants we now regard as weeds flourished, they offered food and medicines.

The term forest does not mean the same as a wood, the distinction is one of ownership. After the Norman invasion in 1066, huge swathes of land became 'forests', only being available to the king and his followers. Those areas were for hunting deer and boar, thus providing meat for the royal table.

Place names in cities reveal a great deal about the land beneath the present-day streets and developments. Looking at the map of London ones sees 'heath', 'marsh', 'green', 'park'. Most significantly is the term 'wood'. The trees too feature, ash, oak, elm, briar, elder and lime. During this recent period of house building planners feel the need to rip out all the existing trees that were getting in their way, and then use names like avenue, grove, copse, belying the fact that there are no trees of any note, other than the saplings newly planted by the landscapers.

The Druids greatly revered the trees in their groves. They understood what some of us are now beginning to understand that trees are living, breathing entities. It has taken man a very long time to see animals in the same way. Man has used them for food, clothing, entertainment and companionship. But the 'dumb' label prevailed. A better knowledge of animals has come to us through the vehicle of television. Sir David Attenborough has brought to the attention of the public, the vast, and often superior knowledge that creatures of all kinds possess; so it is with trees.

Many, many years of forest observation has brought Peter Wohlleben to the conclusion that trees can communicate with one another, they care for one another and sustain each other when there is a need in their community. Trees have a vast underground network to allow this to happen. This information has been verified by scientific research. Trees take a very long time to grow and reach maturity. A glimpse of this is shared in *The Hidden Life of Trees* by Wohlleben. Sadly this knowledge will not the save the destruction of the forests in many places around the world.

Part Two
The History

1.
Beginning of Time

When embarking on this study I did not expect my research to take me on so many journeys. The original aim was to have a better understanding of the medicinal plants found in the acre of a churchyard. All the histories are fascinating. But instead of being relatively simple I found myself asking:

'Who, what, why, where, when and how?'

New scientific studies keep emerging, offering more answers to the past.

Shaman

The earliest 'healers' that are known about are the shamans. Many originated in the vast lands of Siberia, and other northern reaches that are still populated by people known as Sámi. The ancient folk, living in the Palaeolithic Age, had developed the skills of making jewellery and little figurines, particularly of the female form as a sort of deity, or perhaps a fertility symbol. From here it is thought that these groups of people who were hunter/gatherers followed the herds from one continent to another, crossing into what is now North America via the Beringia Ice Bridge to Alaska. The herds of herbivores were necessary to keep them alive, not just for food, but every part of the animal was used for clothing, shelter and tools. The shaman, or healer was a necessary part of the expedition.

Shamans used magic to aid healing. They used a number of herbs that allowed them to access worlds beyond this one. Plants such as psilocybin, today known as 'magic mushroom' could aid such a transition and allow the shaman greater insights through gateways that are closed to mere mortals. Today they still practice in many areas of the world, including Siberia, especially in small towns without a doctor or hospital. Folk still rely on their services. It has been suggested that Rasputin was a shaman. He was very much part of the Russian Orthodox Church; it is a faith that embraces seers, holy men and a variety of mystics and also many versions of Christianity.

It should be said that both the Christian Bible and the Torah (Leviticus and Deuteronomy) denounce shamanic practices.

Druids

When the Romans were invading Britain, reports were made about the Druids, the priests and priestesses who populated the areas in the South of England, the borders of Wales and Gaul (France).

Caesar observed the robed and revered figures of the Druids and portrayed them in a negative light, especially when it came to sacrifices they were said to have made. Pliny was greatly interested in the 'magic' they appeared to practice, and was keen to know about the plants used.

Druids sought seclusion in the woods, and practiced their beliefs in the Groves. Druids revered every living thing around them; the plants, herbs, trees, rivers, springs, rocks, stones and the earth. They could look for answers in the clouds and on the surface of water. Man was very much equal to all of creation.

Being a Druid was a lifelong commitment. Training might last twenty years. All teaching was done orally, discussed and remembered. The written word could be open to misinterpretation. Druids were seers, magicians, poets and shaman. They were judges and law makers.

Druids observed the Celtic festivals of the changing year with feasting and ceremonies. The summer and winter solstices, the spring and autumn equinoxes, Samhain, known as All Hallows or Halloween; Imbolic, Candlemas; Beltaine, May Day eve; and Lugnasad, Lammas. These we would recognise today and are marked in the Christian Church, but celebrated in a different way.

What struck me as being odd about the Druids and Celts was that there were no named persons connected to this period. Culpeper and Gerard were frequently quoted, Dioscorides, Galen and Hippocrates, but not a word about the notable skills of the Celts and Druids. Thanks to Angela Paine's book *The Healing Power of the Celts*, we now know about their amazing skills in the realms of surgery. They perfected the skill of trepanning. This was the procedure of cutting a small hole in the brain to perhaps relive pressure. It was carried out by anaesthetising the patient, using hemlock, mandrake, wild lettuce, ground ivy, eryngo, poppy and orpine. It was evidently successful as recent finds by archaeologists show that the wounds healed and the patients continued to live on for a number of years afterwards. This practice was widespread.

The ogham was the Druid's alphabet. These were a series of horizontal lines either side of an upright line, with some diagonal marks. They could be used on the edge of standing stones or pieces of wood. For example, five horizontal lines indicated the letter N for Nuin, the word for the ash tree and five diagonal marks for R, Ruis, the word for elder. The following trees are found in the churchyard, ash, blackthorn, elder, hawthorn, hazel, holly, ivy, oak and yew.

Celts

The Celts came from the east to Britain 700–650 BC. They were educated and could read and write, both Latin and Greek. The Celts were the farmers, crafts-people, and workers in metals. They settled and lived a rural life, growing fields of corn which were harvested and the grain stored.

Theirs was a simple life; good food, clean water, fresh air, and rest. Everything that we recognise today for a healthy life. However, this departure from the diet of the hunter gatherer would have consequences. Bodies that would have done well on the hunter gatherer diet may not have adapted too well to the new products of grain and milk.

"Our daily bread" (from wheat) became a staple. Milk went into the production of cream, cheese and butter; both would give rise to health problems. Health issues from the past were probably not recognised as being caused by wheat and dairy, but today known and understood as gluten and dairy intolerances.

Modern thinking espouses the idea that the pre-Celtic diet made for healthier people. A great many health conscious people are following the stories in the media of the up to date diets and fads, the Palaeolithic Diet being one.

It has been said that we should eat like cavemen! Not sure about their table manners though…

Some plants that were used in Celtic Medicine are:

Bugle
Burdock
Cinquefoil
Knapweed
Daisy Ox Eyed
Honeysuckle
Mustard
Oak
Pimpernel
Poppy
Primrose
Red Dock
Red nettle
Self Heal
Speedwell
Woodruff

Physicians of Myddfai

These were 13th century Welsh healers. Legend has it that the Lady of the Lake married a mortal. The couple had three sons, the oldest they named Rhiwallon. In time her husband did not please her, and she returned to her home in the lake. However, she did return at intervals to school Rhiwallon in the healing herbs, thus beginning the continuous line of healers until the last Physician of Myddfai died in 1842 at the age of 85 years.

The village of Myddfai, Carmarthenshire in Wales to this day has a connection to the herbs. Those grown today are used to make cosmetics and toiletries.

Shanidar

In recent years the grave of a man known as Shanidar IV was found in a cave in Northern Iraq and labelled the 'flower burial'. It was found to contain the pollen of seven different plants. There is evidence to suggest the cave dates back 60,000 years. There have been suppositions that the man may have been a healer as the flowers can be used medicinally, yarrow, groundsel, St Barnaby's thistle, cornflower, marshmallow, grape hyacinth and hollyhock. Others say that rodents might have taken the plants into the cave. But on the other hand, the man appeared to have been arranged on a bed of yarrow, and the flowers as part of a wreath. It has been said that the hollyhock may have been gathered from a distance (it was a solitary plant) and may have been a special gift for the dead man.

2.
Medieval Fact and Fiction

Fact... Hildegard von Bingen and Trotula of Salerno, Two Remarkable Women

Hildegard von Bingen

During the early Medieval period, two women stood out as being unique. The first was Hildegard von Bingen, born 1098 to a German family of means. Their little daughter had some unusual traits, including visions. At the age of eight she was placed in a Benedictine convent/monastery. In the fullness of time she became the Abbess. With this authority she made some changes. The first and most importantly to separate the convent from the heavily male dominated institution. Hildegard then encouraged woman to join the community, the benefit being a good education. She herself had many talents; poetry, writing, music, composing, indeed a vast collection of interests.

Hildegard was a noted medical healer, and wrote knowledgeably about the workings of the female body. She is credited with writing *Causae et Curae* containing much on the physiology and the pharmacopeia of plants.

The following plants were part of her herbal:

Stinging nettle

"If a man is forgetful and would be cure of it, let him crush out the juice of the stinging nettle, and add some olive oil, and when he goes to bed, let him anoint his chest and temples with it, and do this often, and his forgetfulness will be alleviated."

Mullein

"If any have a weak and sad heart, let him cook mullein with meat or fish, or with other herbs, and eat of them often, and it will strengthen his heart and make it merry."

Hart's tongue

"Hart's tongue is warm, and good for the liver, and the lungs and for pain in the intestines."

Poppy

"It's seeds, if they be eaten, induce sleep and decrease itching. They suppress the torments of lice and nits. They may be eaten boiled in water, but are better and more effective raw than cooked.

Hildegard recognised cancer, and made use of the violet to tackle the growth, and yarrow to stop the initial cancer from metastasising. This thinking was very much ahead of her time!

> For it was that same Love which planted a glorious garden redolent with precious herbs and noble flowers–roses and lilies–which breathed forth a wondrous fragrance, that garden on which the true Solomon was accustomed to feast his eyes.

– Hildegard von Bingen,
letter to the Monk Guibert, 1176

Hildegard died in 1179.

Trotula of Salerno

Trotula of Salerno lived in the 11th or 12th century. She was the first female physician, and said to have been the first female Professor of Medicine, teaching at the medical school, Schola Medica Salernitana in the south of Italy.

Salerno seems to have been a melting pot of medical knowledge from both the east and the west. Texts that were written in Arabic were translations of Greek texts, and those written in Arabic were translated into Latin. Today we know of the writings of Hippocrates, Galen and Dioscorides as a result of this medical college.

Trotula wrote *On the Diseases of Women*. She was what we recognise today as a gynaecologist.

She wrote on all things concerning women from conception to childbirth and everything in between. Regarding infertility, she dared to say that the man might have the problem. She and Hildegard share similar views on sexual relations between a man and a woman. They both agreed that woman should not have to suffer in childbirth. This upset the church, as woman should suffer because of the sin of Eve.

Trotula used a great many herbs to treat the usual ailments, but had a special interest in the cosmetic use of herbs. It can be surprising to know that the women from the past had just as keen an interest in how they looked as we do today. The list is long, here are a few plants that could be used to make one look good, therefore to feel good. too

Agrimony	Hair dye, blond
Barley	Face cream
Barley straw	Shampoo, as a hair mask
Bistort	Skin care ointment, an anti-ageing mask
Cuckoo Pint	Ointment to treat serious skin problems
Ivy gum	Definitive depilation
Mullein	Chelitis (inflammation of the lips), a lipstick to treat
Mustard	Skin lightening, anti-ageing
Oat	Hair dye (blonde)
Violet	Burn plaster, and treatment for cold-damaged skin
Violet oil	Anti-ageing

Women and childbirth

It took the best part of 1,000 years from the time of Trotula for women to be able to practice medicine. Around 100 years ago medical men thought that women using their brains at university would cause their wombs to atrophy.

Hildegard and Trotula were both highly educated particularly when it came to the workings of the female body.

A few centuries later in the Vienna Hospital there was an unusually high number of deaths of healthy young women who had come in to give birth. The cause of death was puerperal fever, a type of sepsis. This was desperately puzzling, as the poorer women who gave births in their homes suffered no such problem. One doctor, Hungarian Ignaz Philipp Semmelweis observed that many doctors would examine dead corpses before coming to aid of the mothers to be. Hand washing was not a big deal, and as often as not, doctors would wear their outdoor clothes when in hospital. Semmelweis made this connection and it was not a popular idea. If the doctors agreed with Semmelweis that their hands should be washed after visits to the morgue, it could implicate them in the many deaths to the mothers that had already occurred. In time it was recognised that hand washing in chlorinated water resulted in bringing down the death toll of mothers. However, Semmelweis was not a popular man. The upset caused him to go insane, and incarcerated in an asylum, he was beaten to death by the guards at the young age of 47 years. Things did change, though slowly, and grudgingly.

Still on the subject of childbirth, one of the first successful caesarean sections to be carried out was in the early 1800s, with both the mother and child surviving. It was expertly conducted by Dr James Barry. He was in fact a woman, and from his teens lived as a man to gain access to the medical schools. He served in much of the British Empire behaving in an exemplarily way, and his/her sexuality only revealed before burial.

And now the fiction... Brother Cadfael

Brother Cadfael came to the Benedictine Order later in life. He was born in Wales in the year 1080. At the age of fourteen he left home to become a servant of a wool trader in Shrewsbury. Two years later he left England to join the First Crusades to the Holy Land, and after a time as a soldier lived in Syria, where he became proficient in the use of medicinal plants.

He returned to England, a land riven with the dispute for the English throne between King Stephen and Empress Maud. By the time he was forty the more peaceful life beckoned, he devoted his life to furthering his knowledge of the herbs, tending the gardens within the walls of Shrewsbury Abbey of St Peter and St Paul.

Author Ellis Peters was meticulous and thorough in her choice of plants. She equipped herself with knowledge on how they would have been used at this time in history.

While within this tranquil place Cadfael worked with the plants, the scribes too did their bit. When not copying religious texts, they were engaged in writing the *Herbals*.

In later years with the Dissolution of the Monasteries 1536–1540 some valuable books from Shrewsbury did find their way into the private collections of the great-great-grandfather of Henry Langley 'Knight of Shropshire'.

Other books were taken to bits and used as good scrap paper, and even second-hand would have been a valuable commodity.

The following is from Owen and Blakeway, *A History of Shrewsbury 1852*, as found in *Brother Cadfael's Herb Garden* by Rob Talbot & Robin Whiteman

> If these actually belonged to our Abbey, the first lay proprietor, Langley, must have been an honourable exception to the great body of such purchasers, who generally sold them to grocers and chandlers. Whole

ship loads, we are told were sent abroad to the book-binders, that vellum or parchment might be cut up in their trade. Covers were torn off for their brass bosses and clasps: and their contents served the ignorant and careless for waste paper. In this manner English History sustained irreparable losses; and it is more than probable that some of the works of Classical Antiquity perished in the indiscriminate and extensive destruction.

Of plants beloved by Cadfael the following have been chosen, taken from the text of Talbot and Whiteman's book:

Anemone also known as Windflower

During medieval times the juice of the Anemone was prescribed externally for leprosy. Mixed with hog's grease, it was used as an ointment for scalds and ulcers. Modern research has revealed that the herb is potentially poisonous.

Moneywort also known as Creeping Jenny

Possessing astringent and antiseptic properties, Moneywort was highly valued by old herbalists as a wound herb. Internally, it was prescribed for stomach and intestinal disorders; and externally for slow-healing wounds, ulcers, skin complaints, and rheumatic aches and pains. Culpeper said "it is good to stay all fluxes, or the flowing of women's courses; bleeding inward and outwardly."

Lilac

Lilac was used in the treatment of fevers, particularly malaria, and to expel intestinal worms. In some parts of

Russia it is still used to rid the body of worms. Elsewhere in Europe it was made into an ointment for rheumatic pains in the joints.

Greater bindweed also known as hedge bindweed

In herbal medicines, both bindweeds were used as a laxative and purgative. Applied externally as a poultice the fresh leaves of the greater bindweed were said to burst a boil within twenty-four hours.

Sow-thistle smooth also known as hare's lettuce

Sow thistle was prescribed for fevers, urinary disorders, stomach complaints, stone, deafness, inflammation, swelling and haemorrhoids. Gerard said that "the juice of these herbs doth cool and temper the heat of the fundament and privy parts." It was also recommended for those that were short-winded and troubled by wheezing.

The end of the monasteries

This peaceful world of healing continued for about 400 years after the supposed death of Cadfael, until King Henry VIII declared that the monks were lazy and worthless, and that the monasteries should close. His coffers were greatly enhanced by the sale/rent of the properties. This process began in 1536 and ran til 1540.

> The dissolution of the monasteries in the late 1530s was one of the most revolutionary events in English history. There were nearly 900 religious houses in England, around 260 for monks, 300 for regular canons, 142

nunneries and 183 friaries; some 12,000 people in total, 4,000 monks, 3,000 canons, 3,000 friars and 2,000 nuns. If the adult male population was 500,000, that meant that one adult man in fifty was in religious orders.

– Professor George W. Bernard

What a loss for the people who relied on these establishments. The Hospice de Beaune in Burgundy gives some idea of what it might have been like to have been cared for in a place that exuded feelings of peace, sense of love and care, not to mention the orderliness and cleanliness of the place.

For the population at large the loss of professional health care must have caused serious problems. Of course day-to-day issues would have been cared for within the home or community. Just as we are familiar with the contents of the bathroom cabinet for storing pain-killers, plasters and cough medicines for instance, our ancestors needed to go no further than the fields surrounding their homes to find the plant remedies. The women in the family generally were the carers.

3.
Tudor and Stuart Times

Herbalism in Tudor and Stuart Times

In the years after King Henry's Dissolution of the Monasteries there was a shift in medical care. Tending the sick fell to the women in the community, usually the older members. Their knowledge was passed down from the older to younger women in the household. What followed next was the emergence of doctors and physicians. University qualifications were required to treat the sick, and with all this superior knowledge, fees had to be charged. Doctors became fashionable and the rich and well to do preferred to be taken care of in this way. Early on in his kingship at the age of 21, Henry set in place 'The Herbalist Charter'. This allowed:

> Men and Women, whom God hath endued with the Knowledge of the Nature, Kind and Operation of certain Herbs, Roots, and Waters, and the using and ministering of them to such as been pained with customisable Diseases, as Woman's Breast's being sore, a Pin and the Web in the Eye, Uncomes of Hands, Burnings, Scaldings, Sore Mouths, the Stone, Strangury, Saucelim, and Morphew, and such other like Diseases; and yet the said Persons have not taken anything for their Pains or Cunning, but have ministered the same to poor People only for Neighborhood and God's sake, and of Pity and Charity:

Six years later in 1518 Henry established The Royal College of Physicians. He had a keen interest in science, but also it seems he cared deeply for his poorer subjects.

Medicine became the preserve of the males. Women were barred from universities, and therefore, without qualifications could not treat the sick. Any that did so may have been perceived as a witch. The far-reaching consequences of this manifested itself two sovereigns later when King James I, the Scottish King, with an irrational fear of witches, wrote a book called *Daemonology*. A year later, in 1604 he persuaded Parliament to pass the Witchcraft Statute, ruling that witchcraft was a crime and would be punishable by death. This in fact lit a slow burning fuse that eventually ended up as the Witch Trials. Those swept across the country during the Civil War forty years later. In East Anglia it reached fever pitch in the hands of Matthew Hopkins. He was a fervent Puritan. It was thought that he may have studied law, as he presented himself well at the trials. Born in Suffolk, son of a Puritan clergyman, Hopkins was twenty-four years of age when he and his colleague John Stearn embarked on this dubious and lucrative career. In 1645 Hopkins proclaimed himself 'Witch Finder General'. The fee of 20/- per town was offered for the services of the young men. It lasted until 1647, when Hopkins died in mysterious circumstances. It may have been that he was thought of as a witch himself.

Not so far away in Essex there is an example of how the larger country houses managed the sick within their community. It fell to the lady of the household to look after her family, servants and farm workers. In 1621 the young bride Elizabeth Winstanley -

prospered at Quendon. She diligently studied cookery and herbal medicine, and quickly gained a reputation for being a very good cook and a skilled physician who could cure most ailments with her herbal remedies. Between 1622 and 1640 she also produced eight children.

– Alison Barnes:
William Winstanley – The Man Who Saved Christmas'

This practice continued for hundreds of years. Manor houses and farming communities could be very cut off from the towns and cities, they had to look to themselves and the healing plants. Elizabeth may have owned a copy of Gerard's *Herbal*!

The four notable herbalists in the Tudor and Stuart times were John Gerard, John Parkinson, Nicholas Culpepper and William Coles.

Of course there were many others too.

All four men were born in the aftermath of the Dissolution of the Monasteries, and therefore those who were sick, out of necessity sought the help of herbalists, or to learn from an herbal how to look after themselves.

From the birth of Gerard 1545 to the death of Coles in 1662, a period of 117 years, a great deal changed. The principle medicines of the day were plant based, and it is interesting to consider what they used them for. Medical conditions were somewhat different, and for most people almost everything was treated without the help of doctors. Disease was rife, poor housing, poor food, bad water and poor sanitation caused much misery. No amount of useful herbs could have prevented many of the illnesses.

John Gerard

John Gerard (1545 – 1612) was the oldest of the herbalists, he published his *Herbal* in 1597. A later version was written in 1633 after his death. This had been revised, updated, and expanded by Gerard's friends.

John Gerard seemed the most controversial character. He surprisingly wrote of the yew that it was perfectly safe to sit among the branches and no harm should befall:

> All that heretofore have dealt in the faculty of Herbarisme, say that the yew tree is very venomous to be taken inwardly, and that if any do sleep under the shadow thereof, it causes sickness and oftentimes death. Moreover, they say that the fruit thereof, being eaten, is not only dangerous and deadly unto man, but if birds do eat thereof, it causes them to cast their feathers and many times to die. All of which I dare boldly affirm is altogether untrue: for when I was young and went to school, diverse of my school fellows and likewise my self, did eat our fill of the berries of this tree and have not only slept under the shadow thereof, but among the branches also, without any hurt at all, and that not one time, but many times.

It would seem that he and his school fellows were educated at Willaston, near Nantwich, Cheshire, and they all lived to tell the tale!

Perhaps unwise to suggest that this plant is safe to be around.

Some wondered if he knew the herbs he was writing about, and sometimes perhaps not. Gerard was a barber-surgeon, and practiced in London. First and foremost he was a botanist, and excelled at raising plants. He was famed for his gardens in Holborn, London. Being recognised as such, he was gifted many foreign and unusual plants to tend. Gerard was superintendent of the gardens owned by William Cecil at the Strand and Theobalds in Hertfordshire.

From 1586 to 1604 Gerard was curator of the Physic Garden established by the College of Physicians. This predated the now famous garden at Chelsea by eighty-seven years.

There are many accounts that suggest he was flawed and very likely plagiarised the work of other herbalists.

John Ray the botanist wrote critically of him, that his work was that of "an ignorant man, and that lacking any foreign languages he could not have translated the work."

In spite of everything Gerard gave the poor people a means of a reference book on how to treat themselves, and copies and notes survived as herbals in the home well into the 20th century, as documented in *Memory, Wisdom and Healing* by Gabrielle Hatfield

Over the many years I have been studying, Gerard is frequently quoted in all sorts of books. The first time his name came to my attention was thirty years ago in Roy Genders, *The Cottage Garden*. This book was a gift from my mother-in-law, a book I truly enjoyed. The quote was on the value of golden rod, it made an impression then, and still does today. It is worth rewriting the whole piece from the Herbal, but I should add that golden rod does <u>not</u> grow in the churchyard, the lesson is in the exclusivity factor of the plant, even although it wasn't!

I have known the dry herb which came from beyond the sea sold in Bucklers Bury in London for half a crown an ounce. But since it was found in Hampstead Wood, even as it were at our town's end, no man will give half a crown for a hundred weight of it; which plainly sets forth our inconstancy and sudden mutability, esteeming no longer of any thing, how precious soever it be, than whilst it is strange and rare. This verifies our English proverb, Far fetch and dear bought is best for Ladies. Yet it more truly said of phantasticall Physicians, who when they have found an approved medicine and perfect remedy near home against any disease; yet not content therewith, they will seek for a new farther off, and by that means many times hurt more than they help. Thus much I have spoken to bring these new fangled fellows back again to esteem better of this admirable plant than they have done, which no doubt have the same virtue now that then it had, although it grows so near our own homes in never so great quantity.

A lengthy piece from Gerard, but something that he made good sense of.

Plants used by Gerard

Goats Beard or **Go to Bed at Noone** *Tragopogon pratensis*

Gerard describes the plant thus:

It shutteth it selfe at twelve of the clock, and sheweth not his face open untill the next daies Sunne doth make it floure anew. Whereupon it was called Go-to-bed-at-noone; when these floures be come to their full maturitie and ripenesse, they grow into a downy Blowball like those of dandelion, which is carried away by the winde.

He mentions the variety that have purple flowers and that grow on the banks of the River Chalder in Lancashire. Those in the churchyard were yellow, therefore resembling the dandelion even more so. It has the same annoying method of spreading itself via the parachute seeds.

As to its virtues, Gerard suggests boiling the roots in wine until tender, and eaten like parsnips, this seemingly "procures that appetite and strengthens those that have been sick of a long lingering disease."

Holm oke *Quercus ilex*

Gerard's description is puzzling. As far as can be known, the holm oak (or holly oak) appeared in England in the late 1500s. He describes the tree as comely, but of little use when it comes to the wood,

He goes on to mention that the

Oke likewise brings forth another kind of excrescent, that the 'Graver' (engraver of the wood cut illustration) has omitted in the figure; Gaza names it *penis*. This penis or prick is hollow, mossy, hanging down half a yard long, like a rag of linen cloth. This Oke carries flowers, clustering upon long stalks, like as in the common Oke; but the fruit does not succeed them, but grows forth in other places.

He quotes Pliny "they bring forth their fruit or Acornes in the fall of the leaf."

(I have to say that I did not observe this fantastical 'excrescent' myself!)

After all that, when it comes to the Temperature and Virtues, he says "We find nothing written of the faculties of this tree among the old writers, neither of our own experience."

Hasell *Corylus avellana*

Better known today as hazel, the parts used are the nuts. Gerard warns that eating the nuts when not quite dry can be difficult to digest, and can "clog the stomach, causing headaches." He suggests that the kernels should be made into milk "like Almonds do mightly bind the belly, and are good for the laske and the bloody flix."

Today hazelnut milk is thought of as a good source of vitamins.

Wilde otes *Bromos sterilis*

Gerard quotes Dioscorides who suggests

> boiling the Otes along with the roots strain, then add to the devotion a quantity of honey equal thereto. Boil until it acquire the thickness of thin honey. This will treat filthy ulcers of the nose, dipping a linen cloth therein and putting it up into the nostrils.

Up to this point the herbs featured by Gerard are used in a fairly conventional way, but there is a surprise to come. After yarrow and yew there comes… The goose tree, barnacle tree, or the tree bearing geese. This notion had been around for centuries. It looked like the chicks did develop from within the barnacles found on rotting wood. Not something we need to worry about as the churchyard is many miles from the coast, but a curiosity none the less.

Finally, the tail piece of the herbal:

And thus having through God's assistance discoursed somewhat
at large Grasses, Herbs, Shrubs, Trees, and Mosses, and
certain Excrescences of the earth, with other things
more, incident to the history thereof, we con-
clude and end our present Volume, with
this wonder of England. For the which
God's name be ever honoured
and praised.
Finis

John Parkinson (1567 – 1650) was a notable botanist and
herbalist. He became apothecary to King James I, and later
Royal Botanist to King Charles I.

Parkinson became the founder member of the Worshipful
Society of Apothecaries in 1617. He was highly respected as
he was exceedingly knowledgeable about plants. His London
home was in Ludgate Hill, and his botanical garden flourished
in the suburbs of Long Acre, Covent Garden. It was probably
two acres in size, where he is recorded to have grown 484 types
of plants, and allowed other gardeners to gather seeds from his
collection. Parkinson kept company with John Gerard, John
Tradescant the elder, the plant collector and others.

Parkinson's great work *Paradisi in Sole Paradisus Terrestris*
gave gardening information on the correct way to grow
plants for the orchard, kitchen and flower gardens in great
detail. This included the methods of grafting, sowing and
planting, how to improve the soil, and the best situations
for the plants to thrive. In 1640 Parkinson produced an
herbal, *Theatrum Botanicum* with 1,688 pages, describing

3,800 plants. It was seemingly the first book to highlight thirty-three native plants, and of course because they were common, they failed to get the recognition they deserved; a point that Gerard made about the golden rod.

This book was a plant identification guide, which would be of help to the apothecary of the day. On presenting a copy to King Charles he was conferred with the title 'Botanicus Regis Primarius' – Royal Botanist of the First Rank.

This tome did not endure in popularity the way that those of Gerard and Culpeper did, probably because of its size. Gerard and Culpeper's herbals were often used in country houses, and indeed recipes from those were frequently copied to be found in the book that the lady of the house might keep her cooking, baking recipes and beauty tips in.

Recently Parkinson's book has been revived by Julie Bruton-Seal and Matthew Seal. They have published the first one, with others to follow.

Pellitory of the wall *Parietaria judaica*

Parkinson used Pellitory for "noises and hummings of the ears", (tinnitus). He found a whole host of uses for it, as a gargle, a treatment for fresh wounds and bruises, a cure for toothache, and it also had diuretic qualities.

Sorrel sour dock *Rumex acetosa*

Parkinson found this a useful plant, as it could be used instead of lemons, to give a tart flavour to food. This can sharpen the appetite especially in cases when a convalescent requires some encouragement to eat. It could also alleviate scurvy. He suggested combining the sorrel with vinegar to treat ringworm and skin infections. An inflammation such as a boil could be drawn to bring about relief. Sorrel could be used to make a thirst-quenching drink.

Lady's bedstraw *Galium verum*

Parkinson recommends this plant for urinary tract infections. It has styptic qualities, for nose bleeds, and as a component of an ointment to soothe burns and scalds. The plant is believed to be carried by weary travellers to help them on their way.

Knapweed *Centaurea nigra*

Parkinson recommends this plant as an astringent to arrest bleeding. It could be used in an ointment to treat bruising, and as a wound healer, to help the two edges of a wound to knit together.

Parkinson suggests that knapweed could be used to prevent mucous from flowing down from the head into the lungs and the stomach.

Nicholas Culpeper (1616 – 1654)

In 2020 366 years after his death, Nicholas Culpeper is still known as the herbalist who wrote a readable herbal to benefit the health of the poor in London. His *Herbal* has never been out of print.

He had an unfortunate start in life. His father a cleric died before he was born. His mother returned to her own home to bring up the child in the vicarage at Ockley, Surrey.

Culpeper was an intelligent boy, and was sent to study at Cambridge where he learned Latin amongst other things.

He became an apprentice to the apothecary Francis Drake. By way of earning his keep he taught Francis Latin. There were many apothecaries in London at that time,

Culpeper married a lady of means, and being financially sound he was able to set up his home and pharmacy at Spitalfields.

There he tended the sick, treating them with the local herbs, and charging nothing or very little for his ministrations. He was disgusted at the medical profession on two counts, the first, they sought out the most expensive ingredients for their cures, and being paid well for their efforts. More importantly they wrote in Latin, and to this end Culpeper decided to write an *Herbal* in English so the ordinary man might understand how to administer treatments for himself. Today Culpeper is still on the bookshelves. I have been gifted two copies; the second with colour illustrations, and a paragraph giving modern uses of the herb featured.

Culpeper was a keen astrologer and enthusiastically prescribed plants that were governed by the planets. He was not the only practitioner to use this method. The Druids also looked to the heavens to consider what plants the planets were related to.

Culpeper worked with the astrologer William Lilly who predicted the King's death, 'A Prophesy of the White King'.

Then came the Civil War. By that time Culpeper had made himself pretty unpopular with the men of medicine, and there were rumours that he practiced witchcraft. It seemed like a good idea to join the king's side, and in 1643 tended the wounded at the First Battle of Newbury. He was shot in the chest, and survived, but was never to return to good health. The new weapons caused new kinds of wounds, never been seen before, resulting in burns and internal traumas. Surgeon Alexander Read wrote, "Man in every age doth devise new instruments of death… we have in our age, *Gun-shot,* the imitation of God's thunder." Sadly, so very true.

Culpeper enjoyed smoking, many men of that period used the new found tobacco for use in pipes or snuff. It is thought that the combination of tobacco and the battle wound affected Culpeper's health, he died at the age of 38 years in January 1654.

Dogs mercury *Mercurialis perennis*

Culpeper roundly states that there is "not a more fatal plant than this." He is critical of Gerard and Parkinson for not cautioning their readers against the use of this plant. There is little more to say on that matter!

This dark plant has a liking for hiding under the hedges.

Yew *Taxus baccata*

Culpeper couldn't agree with Gerard's view that this plant was not harmful. It is indeed exceedingly so. "Its deleterious powers seem to act on the nervous system, but it totally differs from Opium and all other sleep poisons for it does not bring on lethargic symptoms, but penetrates and destroys the vital functions."

Sow thistle *Sonchus oleraceus*

"It is cooling and good against obstructions. The young tops can be eaten in salads with oil and vinegar to ease the pain from scalding urine."

Sloe bush blackthorn *Prunus spinosa*

Culpeper used sloes as an astringent and useful for fluxes and haemorrhages. It makes a good mouthwash and can tone up the gums to help keep loose teeth. The flowers make a purge and can also be used to expel wind.

William Coles (1626-1662)

Coles was the youngest of my chosen herbalists for this period. Of the four he was the youngest when he died, aged 36 years while engaged as secretary to Brian Duppa, Bishop of Winchester.

Coles was born at Adderbury in Oxfordshire. He studied at New College Oxford, from 1642 graduating in 1650 with a B.A. He then went on to obtain his Bachelor of Divinity whilst a fellow at New College. When he was residing for a while in Putney he was the most famous herbalist of his day.

Coles is best remembered for espousing the Doctrines of Signatures, connecting the plants that resembled a certain part of the body, in the belief that they have been ordained by God. Those then identified would be the simples or herb that would be required to heal the problem.

This was not an entirely new idea, going back to the days of Dioscorides and Galen. Paracelsus in the previous century declared that "Nature marks each growth… according to its curative benefit."

Coles wrote *The Art of Simpling', or an Introduction to the Knowledge and Gathering of Plants'* in 1656, and *Adam in Eden, or Natures paradise* in 1657.

His table is called 'Appropriations showing what Part of every Plant is chiefly medicable throughout the whole Body of Man; beginning with the Head'. These are in the correct order that Coles had arranged. Not all the plants are included, only the ones relevant to the churchyard.

Brain	Primrose, cowslip
Head	Poppy
Hair	Mosses
Eyes	Rose, hawkweed
Ears	Ground ivy, ivy, sow thistle
Nose	Wake robin (cuckoo pint), horse tail, shepherd's purse, bistort, tormentil, cinquefoil
Throat	Archangel, foxglove, pellitory of the wall, barley, ragwort, plantain
Lungs	Horehound, coltsfoot, woodbine (honeysuckle), mullein, nettles
Heart	Violet, strawberry, avens
Stomach	Groundsel, daffodils
Stitches	Red clover, oat, stitchwort

Liver	Agrimony, yellow dock, sheep's sorrel, cleavers, chickweed
Spleen	Hart's tongue fern
Kidneys/bladder	Couch Grass, hawthorn, oak, plantain
Dropsy	Elder, bryony, ash
Colic	Holly, bindweed
Diarrhoea	Bramble, pilewort (lesser celandine)
Menses	Mugwort, anemone
Menses/whites	Yarrow, meadowsweet, trefoil, moneywort, hazel
Uterus	Burdock, cow parsley
Childbirth	Holm oak
Hernia	Cranesbill, elm
Wounds/Ulcers	St John's wort, bugle, self heal, daisy, speedwell
Drawing splinters	Pimpernel
For tired feet	Lady's bedstraw

– Source *Matthew Wood MS Registered Herbalist*

How the four herbalists used the plants

The four men were principally botanists and herbalists. They knew their plants and how to treat patients/clients with them. They all shared their knowledge in the publishing of their herbals so all might benefit.

John Ray (1627–1705)

Essex Naturalist – This charming little publication was written by Stuart A. Black, and details John Ray from the time he arrived as the third child on the 27th November 1627. His father Roger was the local blacksmith and his wife Elizabeth lived at Black Notley, near Braintree, Essex.

As a youngster John was taken by his herbalist mother to gather plants she needed to treat the sick in the village. That was when his love of plants was fostered. He was a boy with intelligence and curiosity. From his mother he learned about the medicinal value of the plants being gathered, and how to use them. His studies took him to Cambridge.

Without a proper definition of plants, it would be difficult to determine what plant was needed to treat medical conditions. The following details how plants were identified before Ray's time.

Aristotle (384–322 BC) known as the father of scientific classification, set out his writings based on all that he had learned from the scholars of the past. Theophrastus followed as the father of botany (371–287 BC).

Dioscorides, one time medic to the Roman army became famous for his five volume Greek encyclopaedia, *Materia Medica*. In the volumes were 1,000 entries on treatments many using related substances, but up to 600 medicines were derived from plants. He was both physician and pharmacologist. Dioscorides helped the doctors of the day by organising the pharmacological actions of the drugs to help the doctors. His way of going about the setting out of the plants won the approval of Galen (129-199 AD).

Other notable botanist and herbalists followed, but the first English botanist who devoted his life to the study and classification of plants in a meaningful way was John Ray.

Ray was an earnest student, but by the time he was twenty-three he became ill. It is possible he was suffering from burn out. He had to step back from his studies to recover. As a result of his recuperation he found time to visit the very healing countryside, and rediscovered his love of plants. This led him to begin his studies into the plants and categorise them. It was a project that took him six years of collection and studying, and three to put all the information together into a book. In 1660 his small volume was published, named *Catalogus Plantarium nascentium*, or *Catalogue of Cambridge Plants*.

John Ray's set back in life became a very positive experience, he had the chance to re-evaluate just where he was going, to step back, and change direction.

During the Tudor and Stuart period, individual fields were smaller, about an acre in size, and with the help of oxen could be ploughed in a couple of days. The crops planted were peas, beans, onions and wheat. Potatoes were yet to catch on. These fields would be meticulously weeded by men, women and children. Meadows were part of the agriculture cycle, fields full of grasses and wildflowers grown as a hay crop to feed the livestock over the winter period, and harvested in May/June time. Amongst them might well have been the flowers that Ray recorded. Around the fields the woods and waysides would have been full of many wildflowers and healing plants. One of my greatest joys in recent years was standing in a wildflower meadow, going through the seasons, full of so many amazing plants, and knowing that at one time this is how it would have been.

Individual gardens at that time would have helped sustain the family through the year; crops of vegetables and some salad plants, as well as some medicinal plants, very much the preserve of the women in the house. There were women who made a particular study of herbal medicines, often to be found on the outskirts of the villages, where they were nearer the country spaces, and woods, where they might have a larger area of land to grow their medicines, but also in a good position to seek out particular plants further afield.

Ray was then on a new journey which would eventually have him record plants in the north of England, borders of Scotland and Wales, leading to his 1670 *Collection of English Plants*. Next, *European Plants* in 1673 and *Methods Planerum Nova*, three volumes, 1686, 1688 and 1704.

Philip Miller the Keeper of the Chelsea Physic Garden appreciated this new classification system of the plants in his care. However, it was superseded by Carl Linnaeus's version published 1735–1768.

As a footnote, it can't all be just about the men!

In 1637, widow **Amye Everard Ball**, became the first British woman to register a patent.

She claimed her method of preparing "tincture of saffron, roses &c" would extend the life of these expensive ingredients. Today most herbal preparations are prepared as tinctures.

4.
The Smoking Herbs

Smoking and fuming!

Sir Walter Raleigh was credited with bringing smoking to the English Queen, Elizabeth. What he brought was tobacco, and the notion of using a clay pipe.

It is thought that earliest man having discovered fire might have noticed a pleasant smell when a particular wood or plant material was put into it. This might have caused a sense of well-being, may have provoked spiritual feelings, or helped with some health matter, maybe breathing.

For many thousands of years, shamans practiced medicine and healing with a large degree of magical mysticism. Shamans used herbs in many different ways, herbal infusions, ointments and fumigation. They were used for mind, body, soul and emotions, and often used in ceremonial rituals. Plutarch wrote of the incense used by the Egyptian pharaohs and priests: "The smell of this perfume penetrates your body by the nose. It makes you feel well and relaxed, the mind floats and you find yourself in a dreamy state of happiness, as if listening to beautiful music."

Some herbs found in the churchyard have been useful in the usual way as healing plants, but some are also used for smoking, from the most distant past to more recent times.

It seems really odd to consider smoking anything at all given all, the adverse publicity on the subject today, however, the difference is that unlike cigarettes of modern times, the herbs are devoid of addictive chemicals.

The herbs that could be smoked, from the churchyard (either for inhalation or as incense) are:

Coltsfoot *Tussilago farfara*

Back in Greek and Roman times the leaves were smoked to alleviate a cough or asthma, long before the tobacco plant arrived from the Americas.

In fact even today coltsfoot is known as British tobacco, to help with chest complaints, but often as a substitute tobacco while a smoker is trying to wean themselves off cigarettes.

Mugwort *Artemesia vulgaris*

This is a magical herb, one that can be used in clairvoyance and divination. It is said to bring about prophetic dreams if leaves are placed under the pillow. More down to earth, the smoke might just provide the capacity to clear the scene of annoying insects. It is especially useful as a moth repellent. As a smoke it was used by sailors instead of tobacco or cannabis, and known as sailor's tobacco.

Mullein *Verbascum thapus*

Without doubt a smoking herb, particularly useful for problems of the respiratory tract. For those who prefer to use it conventionally it was used as a country remedy for asthma. It could also be applied as a poultice for chest inflammations.

St John's wort *Hypericum perforatum*

This plant takes its name from John the Baptist, as it flowers around the 24th June, often known as Johns Mass.

It was often burned on an outdoor fire, it seemed to create a feeling of well being. Men were said to jump through the smoke to protect themselves when going off to battle.

Today it can be purchased as a smoking herb, but caution is needed, it is certainly not safe nor should be recommended for everyone.

Sweet woodruff *Galium odoratum*

Woodruff was used by the Physicians of Myddfai for pneumonia and fevers. This plant was used as a strewing herb for the pleasant and fresh aroma that was released upon standing on it.

The following are the findings of the German Commission E Monographs published in 1987: Woodruff is recommended as an herb that could be used to treat diseases and discomforts of the respiratory tract.

It is also a smoking herb.

Cedar *'Cedrus atlantica'*

This ancient tree when used as incense can act as a cleansing agent. It is especially helpful when moving to a new home, as it is said to protect the dwelling of unwanted influences from the past, giving the new residents a fresh start. It is a powerful tree, and can offer protection to a person or place.

And now for something different...

Curiosity took me back to where one expected the smoking to have originated, the continent of America, and the First Americans. It has been discovered that they did smoke the tobacco plant in their pipes, but they also bathed in the smoke from fires, the fires having particular plant material added to them. Illustrations show the sick person lying on a low platform allowing them to inhale the smoke. Also 'sweat lodges' resembling underground saunas were used for cleansing and healing. A fire with the appropriate herbs was kept going while the participants could sweat the impurities out of their systems. Certain leaves can cause euphoria, and a feeling of well being, which is also a form of healing. Pipe smoking too could rid the patient of an infection.

On the other hand, pipe smoking had a very different use, it was used ceremonially, passed between one person and another during a time of reflection, contemplation, and more especially friendship.

In 1804–1806 Captain Meriwether Lewis and Lieutenant William Clark set out on a government sponsored investigation to chart the lands on a fact finding mission; meeting different tribes of the indigenous people. It was a cordial, friendly and peaceful visitation. They were able to record much of the geography. They observed how the Native people lived, how they differed in terms of their dwellings, how they dressed, their artefacts, costumes and customs. As hosts, they welcomed their guests, and were willing to share their peace pipes, a respectful ceremony, done with great reverence, just as the members of the Christian Church might partake in Holy Communion.

Tobacco was introduced to Queen Elizabeth I by Sir Walter Raleigh, along with other goodies from his trips, potatoes, tomatoes and strawberries. These interesting and exotic plants were appreciated for their novelty and were copied, and the drawings used as designs in the decorative embroideries of the day.

The pipes used by the Native Americans when used ceremonially were elaborately carved, perhaps a stone bowl supported by an intricately carved stem. More often though they would have used a clay pipe. It was this that was introduced to the Europeans, and quickly copied.

Various types of smoke have been used across the world, and a way back in time for different purposes. In the preservation of foods, smoking was used to stop meats and fish from deteriorating. In the Middle Eastern desert areas, women cleansed their clothing by supporting them over a conical frame above a low fire with chosen herbs that lightly perfumed the garment, whilst getting rid of moths, and other tiny pests within the fabric. Many churches use incense burners. According to the Book of Revelation: "From the Angel's hand, the smoke of the incense went up before God, and with it the prayers of God's people."

Smoking tobacco having been a ceremonial pursuit became recreational in nature. For many years it was used in pipes, and as cigars and snuff. Then cigarettes were introduced to the masses. Cigarettes became the soldier's friend, and during the Crimean War, Turkish cigarettes were enjoyed.

In southern Spain, Bizet's heroine Carmen worked in a cigarette factory in the 1870s hand-rolling cigarettes. A few years later in 1883 machinery had been developed to enable the production of 600 cigarettes per minute, and sold at five for one penny.

Wild Woodbine cigarettes were first produced in 1888 by W.D & H.O Wills in Bristol and London. The name Woodbine is an interesting choice, the plant woodbine is in fact better known as honeysuckle. It is hard to understand how such a wonderfully scented plant became the name of a cigarette. To add insult to injury the adverts promoting this noxious product featured scenes of beautiful, elegant women surrounded by gardens, and countryside, enjoying the perfume of the woodbine shrub.

How could one fail to be impressed by the idyllic promise of a tempting Woodbine cigarette? Ironically the herbalist Culpeper made use of the honeysuckle for coughs. Honeysuckle was known from as far north in the Highlands and islands, to the very south of England as an herb that could be used to help with breathing problems and asthma. Perhaps Culpeper should have used the honeysuckle, and maybe he did, as he was rather fond of tobacco; between that and a chest wound suffered on the battle field brought about his early death.

During WWI men at the front were sent cigarettes as samples/goodwill gestures. Cigarettes must have been a great source of comfort in that soulless place, and those returning from the front were totally hooked on the white nicotine comforts.

The cigarette manufacturers were the first to offer little collectables in the packets. Cigarette silks as they were known, little satin pictures of First World War generals, national flags, glamorous women; and for the ladies tiny classical paintings by Turner, Rubens, Landseer and many others.

These little satin pieces could be stitched together to make a cushion cover or small quilt. Later cigarette cards were produced of footballers, racing cars and locomotives.

In the USA the tobacco company Philip Morris became the biggest advertiser in the *Journal of the American Medical Association*. Their brand blazed the fact that their cigarettes were "less irritating to the throat." Tobacco manufacturers promoted their wares with slogans "More doctors smoke Camels than any other cigarette." Women suffering from stress were advised by their doctors that smoking would soothe their nerves. Thousands of women responded to the advertisement "Reach for a Lucky instead of a sweet."

Between the wars Hollywood played its part. Glamorous heroines enjoying a cigarette in the company of a tanned and rugged leading man. It was the chic thing to do, and no mention of the potential harm it could do. Cigarette manufactures recognised that smoking caused lung cancer, but few would admit to it.

Along came WW2, and again smoking nicotine seemed to be just the thing to steady the nerves.

It was in the 1930s that there had been observations which linked smoking to lung cancer. In 1947 it was noted that the previous twenty-five years had seen a fifteen-fold increase in the cases of lung cancer in the UK. German researchers in 1939 had made the same observations. In England, Sir

Austin Bradford Hill conducted studies which concluded that smoking was indeed the cause of lung cancer. So the point of this comparison is that although over fifty years ago it was proved irrefutably that smoking caused lung cancer, it is only recently that steps have been taken to ban smoking in public places.

A common saying in Native American country is that when their ancestors first gave tobacco to the European invaders, they knew it was going to kill them, they just didn't think it would take this long!

5.
John Wesley and his Primitive Physick; Erasmus Darwin

John Wesley

John Wesley (1703–1791) is most famously known as a co-founder of Methodism, along with his brother Charles, and George Whitefield.

In 1736 John Wesley sailed to Georgia, in the Americas to spread the word of God to the Native Americans. He deemed the experience a failure and after a few years returned to England where he and his brother preached the Methodist Gospel around the country.

He was a revolutionary preacher, and took religion out of the churches to ordinary people in the countryside preferring to preach beneath a tree standing on a cart to be seen and heard. He and his brother Charles were prolific hymn writers, and most of them still favourites with church congregations. Samuel Wesley provided the powerful tunes to match the rousing words. They were a very scholarly family, John studied at Charter-house School then Christ Church Oxford. He was elected fellow of Lincoln College Oxford.

In her novel *Adam Bede*, George Eliot features Dinah Morris, a young Methodist preacher, a mill girl who has the ability to preach to the masses. Whilst fictional, she remembers the old man with the long white hair who converted her to this new way of thinking. One of the striking things about this new religion was the inclusion of women.

John Wesley cared about the spiritual well-being of his flock, and also of their bodily conditions.

He published the *Primitive Physick, or, An Easy and Natural Method of Curing Most Diseases*. Many of his followers worked in the mill towns, and, having once been country folk now found themselves in places devoid of greenery, never mind healing plants. His philosophy was along the lines of ideas that would be espoused by the naturopaths in later years. This consisted of a simple diet, cleanliness, fresh air, cold baths and exercise. Some of his treatment suggestions are rather odd, one of the treatments he offers for the ague, "Make six middling pills of cobwebs, take one a little before the first fit: Two a little before the next fit: The other three, if Need be, a little before the third fit. I never knew this fail." Spider's webs were part of the medical doctor's treatment of the day. Who knows, this might have some medicinal benefit, but I'm not keen to try it. Another for the common cold, "Pare very thin the yellow rind of an orange," roll it up inside out, and thrust a roll inside each nostril." Could there be something in it? Vitamin C had not been discovered at that point.

Now to the more conventional herbal treatments. John Wesley recommended in his *Physick* the following

Plantain for the bite of a mad dog, flux and cancer of the mouth.

Pellitory of the wall for convulsions of the bowels in children, dropsy, gravel, and pain in the testicles.

Ground ivy for film on the eyes, hot or sharp humours, rash fever and wounds.

Agrimony for gravel, lunacy, bloody urine and putrid wounds.

Groundsel another recommended treatment for ague. Take a handful of groundsel, shred it small, put it into a paper-bag, four inches square, pricking that side which is to be next the skin full of holes. Cover this with a thin linen, and wear it on the pit of the stomach, renewing it two hours before the fit.

Nettle juice was an acceptable cure for "moist Asthma", where it is difficult to breath. Should that fail then tar water, sea water or quicksilver might help.

Wesley gives information on how to use **buttercups** for hemicrania, (severe headaches or migraines). The method of treatment is as follows: "Apply to part of the shaved head a plaster that will stick – with a hole cut in the middle as big as a halfpenny – place over the hole – leaves of ranunculus (buttercup) bruised and very moist.' The resulting blister said to bring about relief.

Later, in Victorian times when blood letting and enemas were part of the medical regimen, they too also used blistering plasters, but instead of buttercups, they made a mixture of cantharides (Spanish fly), euphorbium (the milky sap from the plant genus euphorbia), black pith and yellow resin, yellow wax and olive oil. This plaster was duly applied to the part of the body that was ailing

Wesley suggested two surprising treatments, the first was electric shock treatment for brain/mental illnesses.

The second 'Water-boarding' as recommended by Dr Patrick Blair a Scot, from Boston Lincolnshire. This was particularly recommended for women who might have sought insanity as a way of getting out of an unhappy marriage. Pouring gallons of water from a great height for long periods of time could produce a change of heart. After a couple of weeks of treatment, the woman would be submissive and willing to return to her husband.

Water-boarding treatment was a favourite of the Spanish Inquisition, so it was a fairly common torment.

Unfortunately both those seemingly unpleasant treatments are still in use, water-boarding is used as a form of torture, while the use of electroconvulsive therapy, ECT, is used in the USA to help children with mental problems.

John Wesley was a very generous man, in 1746 he opened up dispensaries in London and Bristol to treat the suffering, at little or no cost. Those who had left the countryside behind would have valued the availability of the plant medicine.

Dr. Erasmus Darwin

In the middle years of the 1700s doctors were few and far between. Charles Darwin's grandfather, Erasmus was a very successful doctor, who may well have seen the great Methodist gatherings conducted by John Wesley. Of course, very few could have enjoyed the benefits of a visiting doctor. Dr. Darwin travelled a great many miles daily to visit patients. In his brightly painted carriage he carried all he needed, medical books, potions, instruments, and very importantly sustenance for himself. He liked the finer things in life, and his food hamper was replete with cold meats and fine wines.

In the days before tar macadam and long before the rubber tyre, travelling by coach must have been really uncomfortable. Dr. Darwin however improved the basic coach design by developing a better steering mechanism, and better axles. More importantly, he invented spring suspension. Those developments should have ensured a better dining experience!!

Dr. Erasmus belonged to the scientific group known as the Lunar Men. He was a contemporary of Dr. William Withering.

6.
Foxgloves and Dr. William Withering (1741–1799)

It should be no surprise that the young William Withering should choose a vocation in medicine. He was the son of an apothecary, and nephew of two physicians. His home was in Shropshire, England. At the age of twenty-one he chose to study medicine in Edinburgh. The Medical School was established in 1726. It soon became THE place to study medicine, a reputation based on the standing of the tutors, considered the best to be found. Withering studied neurology with Robert Whytt, chemistry with Joseph Black, and anatomy with Alexander Monro.

The young Mr Withering was greatly impressed by the classes in clinical medicine tutored by Dr. William Cullen (later to become professor), who was famous well beyond the United Kingdom. Indeed, Dr. Benjamin Rush travelled from Philadelphia USA to be one of his students.

Edinburgh held the key for progressive medicine in the post-Newtonian days.

Withering had a great interest in plants, and while in Edinburgh may well have been familiar with the Botanical Garden set up for the purpose of finding out about the medicinal properties of plants. This was established in 1670, after the Oxford Botanical Garden, and before the Chelsea Physic Garden in 1673. This facility enabled the medical students to further their knowledge of herbalism.

Dr. Withering graduated in 1766 as physician and started in private practice in Stafford. When there he met patient Helena Cooke who shared William's love of plants and to help her recover William gathered the best flowers he could find to allow her to paint them. In 1772 they became man and wife.

Plant identification

One of the earliest books on plant identification was written by John Ray. Later in 1735 the Swede Carl Linnaeus published his version of plant classification, *System Naturae*. What made this classification so ahead of its time was the fact that Linnaeus had noted the sex of the plants, the male and female and the role of each to the production of seeds for the continuance of the species. The terminology seemed rather rude, and not what well brought up ladies should be exposed to. This seemingly caused great offence to Dr. Withering, so that he produced his own! He published *A Botanical Arrangement of All the Vegetables Growing Naturally in G. Britain* (1776), then *An Arrangement of British Plants* (1787–1792). Much more suitable for the ladies.

Dr. Withering had a great interest in plants, but he did not think of them in medical terms, believing that their usage showed both ignorance and superstition!

At the end of the day it is the Linnaeus system that prevails.

In 1783 the second *Edinburgh Pharmacopoeia* was published, nearly a century after the first one, this incorporated the scientific findings of the plant's constituents, which in many cases confirmed the empirical usage of a particular plant.

By comparison the doctor's *Materia Media* of the day resembled more the collection of the bits that Macbeth's witches might have used... Spanish Fly, pigeon blood, elk's hoofs, dung of peacock, pig and horse, spider's webs, eggs of ants and spawn of frogs!

In 1775 Dr. and Mrs Withering moved to Birmingham. This came about upon the death of Dr. Small, and at the suggestion of his friend Erasmus Darwin, William took up the post vacated by Dr. Small.

Dr. Small was a key member of the group known as the Lunar Men, this was the name by which a group of amateur scientists were known.

The initial group was formed of John Whitehurst, Matthew Boulton, Josiah Wedgwood, Erasmus Darwin, James Keir, Richard Edgeworth and Thomas Day. This was the period of many scientific discoveries, not in universities, but between groups of friends with similar interests. The term 'Lunar' was appropriate as they used the light of the full moon to travel to their meetings. On the Monday nearest the full moon, they met at one another's houses, starting with lunch at 2 pm, then going on to debate all things of scientific interest to them before getting into their carriages at 8 pm to get them safely home. The extra light afforded by the full moon must have helped on the journey.

In time, others joined the group, James Watt, Samuel Galton, Joseph Priestly and William Withering becoming members. They were some of the finest scientists of their time. Many of those men are remembered today for their contributions to the sciences.

As an aside it is interesting to note that Charles Darwin's grandfathers were Erasmus Darwin and Josiah Wedgwood.

Withering had a thriving practice in Birmingham, said to have been the largest in the area. He conducted clinics for the poor, free of charge at the Birmingham General Hospital. He also liked to visit his infirmary patients in Stafford. This involved a thirty-mile journey, and halfway the horses needed to be changed. On one such occasion Withering was asked to look at a very sick woman, with dropsy, also known as oedema. It seemed unlikely she would make a good recovery, but, amazingly she did. The patient had been treated by a Shropshire herb woman, and Withering observed that out of the twenty or so plants in the treatment, the most likely element was the Foxglove. Thereafter he worked on research to refine and hone the preparation. The active ingredient in a plant might be the fruit, the bark, the root, and in this case, Withering decided that the leaf gave the most consistent results. By drying the leaf and pounding it down to a fine powder it was ready for use.

Dr Withering used 156 of his own patients to demonstrate the efficacy of the plant. He followed this up with *An Account of the Foxglove and its Medicinal Uses*.

The foxglove is a dangerous plant unless it is used with caution, the right dosage is essential.

The following quote seems expedient here:

> The physician does not learn everything he must know and master at high college alone; from time to time he must consult old women, gypsies, magicians, wayfarers, and all manner of peasant folk and random people, and learn from them, for these have more knowledge about such things than all the high colleges.
>
> – Paracelsus

7.
Homeopathy: Less is More

Dr Christian Friedrich Samuel Hahnemann (1755-1843)

Dr Edward Jenner (1749-1823)

This is the story of two men and their amazing discoveries. One is Dr. Christian Friedrich Samuel Hahnemann born 1755 in Meissen Saxony, son of a designer of the very fine porcelain for which the town is famed.

The other Dr. Edward Jenner born 1749 in Berkeley, Gloucestershire, and son of the local vicar.

Dr. Hahnemann

As a young man Hahnemann excelled at languages, mastering Greek, Latin, English, French and Italian. He made a living teaching and translating, eventually adding Hebrew, Syriac and Chaldaic to this already impressive collection.

He then chose to study medicine, first in Leipzig, then Vienna, and graduated with Honours from the University of Erlangen with an MD. His thesis was on 'The Causes and Treatment of Spasmodic Diseases'. This was followed by taking up a position as village doctor in Saxony. Marriage and eleven children followed. He became disillusioned with the accepted medical treatments of the day, and noted that the patients did not flourish. Hahnemann returned to his previous profession using his language skills. This was to bring about the most amazing changes in his fortunes.

Professor William Cullen engaged Hahnemann to translate his *A Treatise on the Materia Medica*. Cullen was a prominent Scottish physician and chemist. At that time the Edinburgh Medical School was at its zenith and Cullen was greatly revered. He was very much a central figure within the Scottish Enlightenment.

Professor Cullen at one time was President of the Royal College of Physicians and Surgeons of Glasgow, President of the Royal College of Physicians of Edinburgh and First Physician to the King in Scotland. Also Cullen was instrumental in acquiring a royal charter for the Philosophical Society of Edinburgh, which resulted in the formation of the Royal Society of Edinburgh in 1783.

In choosing Hahnemann, Cullen had the benefit of not just a translator, but a fellow doctor who would understand his work.

In his *A Treatise on the Materia Medica* Cullen stated that cinchona, otherwise known as Peruvian bark, due to its astringent properties was an effective treatment in malaria.

Curiosity led Hahnemann to test this on himself, and he experienced malarial type symptoms. Then came his Eureka moment. The realisation "that which can produce a set of symptoms in a healthy individual, can treat a sick individual who is manifesting a similar set of symptoms."

Hahnemann's phrase "let likes cure likes" became the hall mark for his exciting discovery which he named homeopathy.

Clinical Trials

In 1986 trials were conducted in the Glasgow Homeopathic Hospital carried out by Dr. D.T. Reilly and his team. The result dismissed the notion that it was a placebo effect.

Homeopathy works by getting to the bottom of the illness and treating accordingly, rather than suppressing the original problems. Also homeopathy is successful in the treatment of animals who really have no idea what they are being given.

Today it is recognised around the world as a treatment that is safe and effective.

Dr. Edward Jenner (1749-1823)

Edward Anthony Jenner at the amazingly young age of fourteen was apprenticed to a local surgeon, followed by his medical training in London. Having qualified, he returned to his home town to practice medicine. His story is one well remembered from my primary school days. Such a famous and inspirational account of how this young doctor observed the fact that milk maids rarely suffered from smallpox, a scourge of a disease.

Jenner noted that milk-maids often suffered cowpox, but rarely got smallpox. Could this lead to the answer? After all, the old wives' tales said that milk-maids who contracted cowpox rarely caught smallpox. Smallpox was a scourge in many parts of the world.

Ideas around the protection from smallpox as used by the Asians and Africans, seemed primitive, but effectual. The method was blowing small dried pox scabs up the nose of the patient. It was known as variolation. As an improvement on this technique powdered scabs were rubbed into a small cut on the skin. It seemed to have been effective.

Jenner decided he should use the pus from a cowpox blister and administered this via a small nick in the arm to 'inoculate' against the smallpox. His guinea pig was eight-year-old James Phipps. The rest is, as they say, history!

This is just a small taste of the fascinating story of Edward Jenner's life, but one that is similar to the story of Hahnemann. Edward Jenner initially suffered much hostility to his treatment, and indeed ridicule. The popular artist of the day, James Gillray couldn't resist sending up this new piece of medical science. He painted a gathering of people being inoculated showing cows growing out of their bodies: *The Cow Pock or The Wonderful Effects of the New Inoculation.*

In Jenner's case in the fullness of time his vaccine became a boon to the prevention of smallpox.

When going through some family papers, I found my grandfather's Compulsory Vaccination Act – Schedule, dated 1873. It was a two foolscap document, on blue paper and signed by Dr. White, the Vaccinator of the Parish. The vaccine one assumes was smallpox, but not stated on the document. At that time vaccination was compulsory, with fines or prison sentences imposed for those wishing to avoid it. Variolation became illegal in 1840. The term vaccine came into being, from the Latin for 'cow'.

Hahnemann

Dr. Jenner succeeded, and was lauded for his efforts. It was not the same for Hahnemann. His initial successes gave way to the spite and hostility of the medical profession, and the apothecaries. He was ridiculed. He seemed finished. At the age of seventy-five his wife died. Then, a young lady from Paris visited him, a devotee of his work. In no time at all he married the young Marie Melanie d'Hervilly, some forty years his junior They left for Paris. Homeopathy was well received in France.

Now, it is an interesting thing that today in the European Union, homeopathy is just one of the accoutrements of the European doctors. They are medical doctors first and foremost, they also practice complementary and alternative medicine (CAM). A patient can have an appointment and be offered homeopathy, acupuncture, osteopathy, chiropractic, herbalism, whatever is most suitable to their well being. In the United Kingdom the NHS positively refutes that there are any medical benefits in homeopathy. Having said that, doctors in private practice will accommodate whatever their patients would like.

It is interesting to see that Queen Elizabeth II, Prince Philip and Prince Charles all endorse homeopathy. The first royal to espouse homeopathy was the wife of King William IV, Queen Adelaide. (1792–1849). The Marquess of Anglesey sought treatment from Dr Hahnemann himself. Today the Royal Seal of Approval is granted to Ainsworth, supplier of homeopathic preparations.

Now to some of the remedies. As a Bach Flower Practitioner, I do understand quite a bit about how the remedies work, but they are still quite complex to understand.

It is more than just treating the ailment, it is understanding the person's mental and emotional state. Then there are Modalities, whether the pain/condition is better or worse given certain situations. Many of us can relate to seeing two different people with the same medical condition, but how they behave in the given circumstances can be very different.

American Oliver Wendall Holmes(1809-1894) physician and writer, is quoted as saying that it was not enough to treat the man as he presented himself, but if one could know his background, see his home life, the happiness or lack of it, financial situation, there might be a clue to the man's ill health.

Finally, today the latest buzz word is 'micro-dosing'. This is becoming accepted when using magic mushrooms. It seems like homeopathy by another name!

8.
Sweat Lodges

Sweat lodges have a place in northern hemisphere cultures.

There are claims suggesting that the Native Americans were the first to have them, it might be true. It would seem however that origins go back to shamanic times and being close to Mother Earth, as a way of living and healing. A sweat lodge could be made out of the earth, usually beside a lake or stream. The internal space allowed for a fire of wood or peat, and could accommodate a single person, or a few sick people. It is a primitive notion, and therefore it is impossible to say who thought of it first! It is true that folk in Finland and Sweden have enjoyed such a thing as part of their culture.

It is timeless; the Romans, the Japanese and Chinese had their own versions of saunas.

In the United Kingdom there is evidence of sweat lodges, but known as 'burnt mounds' in the Shetland Isles, so called because of the mystery of discovering shattered stones. New thinking does link them to the sweat lodge tradition, the ritual cleansing by either dry heat or moisture; in this case causing the fire heated stones to shatter in the trough of water. Burnt mounds were also discovered in Birmingham England, and estimated to be 3,000 years old.

In Ireland they are dotted around near to the hamlets and villages, and can blend into the surroundings that they might not be recognised.

Very often they are only large enough for one. A small oval or circular space is dug out of the hillside, and the roof constructed of turf and flat stones. The entrance is tiny, meaning that those who were passing in or out needed to crouch very low. The space would be prepared beforehand: a fire lit on the bare ground, and when a suitable temperature was reached, and the fire had burned out, the helper to the sick person would crawl in and sweep out the ashes, ready for the patient. Thereafter, the entrance was closed up. Someone would remain outside in case the sick person needed help. On leaving the lodge it was usual to bathe in a pool of water.

In 1794 horticulturist Charles Whitlaw visited America and made an interesting discovery.

Whilst in the company of the Native Americans, he witnessed the success of their way of sweating out an illness or infection. It was done thus, by arranging a few stones and surrounding them with a small tent like structure. Herbs and some water were dropped onto hot stones, and one or more persons sitting around to benefit from the procedure.

Whitlaw tried it himself. He was smitten by the idea. On returning to England in 1820 he set up vapour baths, and, like the Native Americans, used selected herbs for the best effects. He set up the baths in London, Manchester, Poole, Hastings and a number of other places, including his home town of Edinburgh where he had commenced his studies. Within ten years he had treated over 60,000 cases, with success. The popularity of the vapour baths lasted only as long as Whitlaw did. On his death this business ceased without someone with Whitlow's enthusiasm to carry it forward.

Sometime later Turkish baths appeared on the scene. Harrogate was to become famous for the opulent tiled domed ceilings and walls. Opened in Victorian times wealthy patrons flocked to sample the waters, and experience the 'baths' as they were known.

Today a great many leisure centres offer steam rooms or saunas.

9.
The Shakers and their contribution to herbalism

This story starts not in America, but in England, in the Black Country 'Cottonopolis', otherwise known as Manchester. During the mid-1770s this was a horrendous place to live, or just exist. The majority of people were put to work in the misery of the cotton production, long hours, poor wages, and forced to live in the squalor of cramped houses, amid piles of human waste. Only one person in twenty-eight made it to their fortieth birthday.

At this time there was a move away from the conventional religion; the Quakers and Methodists flourished. Both allowed equality of the sexes, men and women worked together, sharing the responsibilities and decision making.

Out of this ghastly place there emerged a woman who had a vision of a better life, Quaker Ann Lee. At the age of thirty-eight, having been married, had four babies, none of whom survived, she decided that America should be her new home. In 1774 she and eight others set sail on 9th May, on the Mariah, arriving at New York on the 6th August after a very stormy time at sea. This journey was longer than the *Mayflower*'s crossing in 1620 by twenty-four days.

Their faith must have been strong to endure such a crossing.

Once there, the men in the party set out to find suitable land for their purposes, to grow the herbs that they had brought from England. Of course, this was initially for their own use, a wise precaution if they hoped to survive.

They settled at Watervliet seven miles north west of Albany. With help from friendly natives, they learned how to tend the land and grow the crops they needed to survive. The little community flourished, and as successful gardeners, they sold their surplus.

Their forte was growing medicinal herbs, and as business people they were able to make a good living through their own hard work. Their fame spread and they were able to send dried herbs and seeds through the post to clients. There was a good postal system in the USA thanks to the efforts of Benjamin Franklin.

With the passage of time there were a number of Shaker centres, all with the same ethos; all supplying herbs to both the conventional and the Eclectic doctors, and to the pharmaceutical companies.

The Shakers promoted themselves using seed and preparation catalogues for mail order. Those were shipped to England, Belgium, Germany, Italy, Spain, Australia, Constantinople, Greece, India and Africa. Their most popular line was a medicine for dyspepsia. In three years, they shipped five million bottles to London.

Having started off in such a small way in 1775, the Shaker enterprises were at the height of their successes between 1820 – 1850. With the 1860s came the Civil War. The Shakers cared for the soldiers from both sides who came to their doors. One huge problem the Shakers did have – they were celibate. Therefore, there was no succession. They kept going by adopting children into their way of life. During a cholera epidemic, children surviving their parents were taken into the safe-keeping of the Shaker community.

What about the plants?

Folk were settling from Europe in the early 1500s, they introduced plants from their homelands. They took many herbs for a great number of maladies. Good health was essential to succeed.

By the time the Shakers arrived plants from the old world had naturalised. It would be perfectly sensible to travel with the plants known to the travellers. One in particular known as white man's foot was the plantain. Wherever the white man went, there was evidence of his visit thanks to this useful little plant taking root.

Introduced, naturalised and native plants

There are a great many plants within the Shaker botanical lists that actually originated in Britain.

Of the ones found in the churchyard, I have chosen the following and how the Shakers used them.

Agrimony

Highly recommended in bowel complaints, gravel, asthma, coughs and gonorrhoea. Used as a tea sometimes infused with liquorice root. Also used as a gargle for throat and mouth irritations.

Burdock

Used in gout and scorbutic, syphilitic, scrofulous and leprous diseases; the leaves are used as a cooling poultice. The root should be dug in the fall or early spring. Only year-old roots should be used. Externally, it is valuable in salves or as a wash for burns, wounds, and skin irritations.

Ox-eye daisy

Used in whooping cough, asthma, nervousness, and leukorrhea, and as a local application to wounds and cutaneous diseases.

Ground ivy

A stimulant, tonic and pectoral. An infusion of the leaves is very beneficial in lead colic, and painters very often make use of it. The fresh juice sniffed up the nose often relieves nasal congestion and headache. Used in diseases of the lungs and kidneys, asthma and jaundice.

St John's wort

Used to cure suppression of urine, chronic urinary afflictions, diarrhoea, dysentery, worms and jaundice. As an ointment used for wounds, ulcers, caked breasts and tumours.

Lowly Worms

A little paragraph caught my eye, 'Scolding Worms to Death'.

The Shakers kept extensive records of what happened on a day to day basis. This came from the diary entry on 4th June 1806. Farmers at that time thought that worms were harmful to the crops, so they attempted to eradicate them. "Oliver kills the worms in the garden. Sister Ruth gathers two quarts of worms, but will not kill them and so she scolds them to death."

This statement is hard to verify. I hope Sister Ruth scolded them rather than scalding them!

The Shakers expressed their love of God through their ecstatic dance moves, known as Shaking. They delighted in the gifts bestowed on them by God Almighty. The Shakers were musical, and produced a Hymnal. They gave us the beautiful well-known hymn, 'Simple Gifts'. It is better known now to the lyrics of Sydney Carter, as 'Lord of the Dance'.

A blade of grass – a simple flower
Cull'ed from the dewy lea;
These, these shall speak with touching power
Of change and health to thee.

– From the New Lebanon Shakers' 1851 catalog.

10.
The First Americans

The Americas were discovered by Christopher Columbus in 1492, thus beginning the voyages of many other explorers from Europe, all seeking new land and treasures. This became known as 'The New World'.

On their arrival many commentators wrote about the fine physique and well being of the Native Americans. They were upright, strong, exceedingly healthy, and, all in all, a very fine body of people.

The first settlers were welcomed by the Natives, and indeed the Huron people treated sailors arriving on their shores for scurvy.

When the settlers of the *Mayflower* arrived in 1620, they did not receive a warm welcome. The indigenous people had suffered appallingly at the hands of the Europeans, plus they found themselves sick and dying of the new diseases that they did not have the immune systems to cope with, nor did they have the herbs to deal with the new sicknesses.

It is recorded that, on the whole, the indigenous people were friendly and willing to get on with the 'visitors'.

A century later Mother Ann Lee was treated very hospitably by the local people. They introduced her to their healing plants which became part of the Shaker pharmacopeia.

Of the illness introduced, 'smallpox' was the gravest. The

Native Americans tried to cure themselves using the sweat lodge method, up until then the notion of sweating out an illness had worked, but in the case of smallpox this did not help. It caused dehydration, and as part of the treatment, a plunge into cold water shocked the system, leading to cardiac arrest. It also infected others. They learned instead to adopt quarantine measures. This malaise did not go unnoticed by the British Army and led to the practice of what might have been termed the first biological warfare. It is said that Lord Jeffrey Amhurst, commander in chief of the British forces in North America, advocated giving the Natives blankets and handkerchiefs infected with smallpox. These gifts were gratefully received.

Sadly the European diseases killed up to 90 percent of the Native Americans.

– Source of Small Pox, Jesse Greenspan

European plants entering the Native American pharmacopeia

Through time there was an acceptance of European plants and how they might be used by the indigenous people. In exchange there were benefits of the American plants brought back by the Europeans.

The following examples come from *How Indians Use Wild Plants for Food, Medicine & Crafts* by Frances Densmore.

Chippewa Indian Reservations

The plants so familiar in England found their way into the

Pharmacopeia of the Chippewas. Studies were carried out in 1926–1927.

The identification and the meanings and uses are very simple. Here are a few of them

Yellow dock *Rumex Crispus*
Meaning – 'pike plant' use – eruptions (we can only guess)

Avens *Geum canadense*
Meaning – (not stated) use – diseases of women

Burdock *Arctium minus*
Meaning – bitter leaf use – cough

Shepherds purse *Bursa pastoris*
Meaning – 'fire root' use – dysentery

Puffball *Calvatia craniiforum*
Meaning – (not stated) use – nose bleed

Smart Weed *Polygonum persicaria*
Meaning – (not stated) use – pain in stomach

Lost in translation!

The most interesting plant for me here is the 'smart weed', also known as red shank, arsemart, *Polygonum persacaria*

One of the first books I used when starting this writing project was Culpeper's *Colour Herbal* giving the information as per his original book. Going through plant by plant I ignored arsemart as probably a foreign plant and unlikely to be growing in the churchyard.

Then when reading the Scot's *Herbal*, it appeared under Persicaria redshank, which did grow in the churchyard mainly in the gravel path. The Scottish name was arsemart or spotted arsemart.

The Gaelic name means 'herb of the crucifixion tree', so called because it was said to have been growing under the cross of Christ and the leaves were marked with His blood.

According to Culpeper there are two similar plants, one "the Hot Arssmart is called the Water-pepper. The mild Arssmart is called Dead Assmart, or Peachwort." Culpeper wrote: "Our college Physicians mistake the one for the other in their New Master-Piece, whereby they discover their ignorance, their carelessness; and he that but half an eye may see their pride without a pair of spectacles."

He did not write kindly of the doctors. Writing of the "Mild Arssmart" he recommends it for putrid ulcers, worms, toothache, inflammations and green wounds. It is not clear to me which arsemart he is talking about in the following he appears to suggests that "if you will be pleased to break a leg of it across your tongue, it will make your tongue smart."

I guess it may well cause smarting at the other end of the alimentary canal too!

Looking at plants as used by the Chippewa Indians, Polygonum persicaria has the common name 'smart weed' for pain in the stomach. This plant from Britain and Europe, naturalised in the USA found its way into the Native American pharmacopeia. It certainly looks like arsemart became smart weed!

This story appeared in the *Financial Times* in 2006 regarding the purchase of Hard Rock International by the Seminole Tribe. A generation before they had suffered great poverty. They did in fact turn this around by allowing gambling on their reservations. With the huge sums they accrued they were in a position to make this purchase. A spokes person for the Seminoles is quoted as saying, "Our ancestors sold Manhattan for trinkets…now we are going to buy Manhattan back, one hamburger at a time"!

When the Last Tree Is Cut Down,
the Last Fish Eaten,
and the Last Stream Poisoned,
You Will Realise That You Cannot Eat Money

11.
Thomsonians

Back and forward across the pond

Until the 1880s Britain had been supplied with herbal products from the Shakers. Many of the plants used in the preparations would have originally come from England in the first place, being introduced by the earliest settlers. Combined with the indigenous native plants they formed the Pharmacopeia of the Shakers.

Samuel Thomson

Samuel Thomson (1769 – 1843) To this day Thomson is known for having made discoveries that enabled the masses to have a better understanding of how they could achieve good health for themselves and their families. He was a very poorly educated man who chanced upon a plant that could rid the body of 'obstructions'. This was lobelia, and in conjunction with cayenne pepper made a 'cure-all'. He also promoted steam as a treatment, relating that his tiny daughter was close to death when he hit upon the idea of holding her over steaming water until her body relaxed and she could breathe properly again. Thomson perfected a way of providing his herbal remedies to the millions, this he did effectively by training agents to sell his products. He wrote papers to be sold with the herbs giving the information needed to self-treat. Thomson set about putting a repository in every city and major town in the USA. From there the herbs were distributed.

There were major events taking place in the United States. In 1803 the Louisiana Purchase was made, potentially opening up the wild west. The Lewis–Clark Expedition mapped out the route from St Louis to the Pacific, following the Missouri, Yellow and Columbus Rivers. The life that beckoned the pioneers would be extremely harsh, a voyage into the unknown. Thomson helped every man and his family to help themselves, and he gave them instructions on how to do so. With many folk keen to settle into the newly available land there was a great up take of Thomson's self-help herbal, *The System of Botanical Practice of Medicine*. His agents publicised and promoted this on his behalf. Customers had to buy into the system.

For the families taking the 'System' into their new world, many must have owed their lives to this support. Old photos show images of families standing outside their turf-built houses, looking gaunt, just struggling to survive. And survive they did, and many flourished there.

In 1813 the Native Americans offered *The Indian Doctor's Dispensary* in Cincinnati, with their own herbal remedies. "The natives of our own country are in possession of cure, simples etc. that surpass what is used by our best practitioners."

The Native Americans also used lobelia and steaming.

By 1839 Thomson had three million followers/clients.

Samuel Thomson does have a legacy, he influenced a great many people, and still to this day it is so. The Herbalist Dr. John Christopher continues to promote the teachings of Thomson. Indeed today Melanie Cardwell of Herbcraft Academy recommends the use of lobelia and cayenne, another fan of Dr. Thomson and Dr. Christopher.

Thomson had a meeting with Dr. Benjamin Rush of Philadelphia a nationally acclaimed physician, in the hope that he would support his ethos.

Rush was interested, but perhaps not supportive, he had urged his students to "converse freely with quacks of every class and sex... you cannot imagine how much a physician with a liberal mind may profit from a few casual and secret visits to people."

Dr Rush was a signatory of the Declaration of Independence, 4th July 1776.

With the passage of time Thomson's star was on the wane, he became distrustful and jealous of those around about him. He had reached the giddy heights of adulation and success, and is remembered for his use of lobelia to cleanse the body through vomiting.

In 1825 Dr. Hans B Gram returned to his homeland Denmark to study, and brought back something new, homeopathy. This caused uproar amongst the medical fraternity, but the new treatments were extremely popular with the Americans.

Dr. Wooster Beach (1794–1859) a qualified doctor, emerged embracing a number of treatments that were not mainstream; he called this mixture 'Eclectic'; some conventional, some alternative, basically a pick and mix system of treating the patient with what suited them. Eclectics promoted homeopathy and Thomson's treatments which included 'sweating' and Dr. Beach's take on the gentle care for the patients.

Dr Beach became the President of the National Eclectic Medical Association in 1855.

From the USA Dr. Albert Isiah Coffin (1790-1866) sailed to England. He was on a mission to spread the word about herbal medicine to the English, arriving in 1838 to a London that was not yet ready for him. The northern towns and cities were more deserving of him. The populous took him to their hearts. He was first and foremost a dealer in herbs in the Thomsonian tradition, but he was also an entertainer, a showman who loved an audience. Hardly one to hide his light under a bushel he promoted his lectures with posters ahead of his performance in all the major halls. His stock was basically Samuel Thomson's mixtures with lobelia and cayenne. He also used the European herbs agrimony, cleavers, and pellitory of the wall. Much of his stock was supplied from the Shakers in America.

In the fullness of time Coffin was succeeded by some homegrown talent…

John Skelton (1805 – 1880s)

John Skelton was born in Devon, England in 1805. As a small boy he delighted in spending time with his maternal grandmother Mary Edwards. He helped her to gather herbs she would go on to use on the sick people she cared for. Mary's gravestone bears the inscription, "For many years skilful doctress and midwife of the village."

Skelton did not forget the teachings of his grandmother, and whilst still a boy he overheard a Scotsman asking where he could get some pellitory which he needed for urinary problems. The young lad was happy to speak up and say that he knew where some could be collected, he did so and was rewarded with sixpence.

Little is known of his early life, but it became apparent that he was working alongside Dr. Coffin, as in 1848 he is featured in Dr. Coffin's *Journal* advertising the fact that he was lecturing, and consulting in Blackburn, Heywood and Bradford.

Dr. Coffin, in the Thomsonian tradition, engaged a number of acolytes to spread the word, and this is how Skelton became involved. Before becoming an herbalist in 1848, he had been an active Socialist, a member of the London Working Men's Association and a signatory of the People's Charter. Skelton championed democratic values.

Skelton made studies of the indigenous herbs as well as those that were being imported from the Americas and the Colonies. In 1836 he qualified as a medical practitioner and later published *Science and Practice of Herbal Medicine* (1870) for use by students of herbal medicine.

What is of great importance was the influence he had on others, it is thought that as a result of his lectures John Boot (1815–1860) opened his store in Goose Gate, Nottingham. He too was an herbalist. After his death, his son took over the business selling herbal preparations, and the newer medicines of the day. In twenty years Boots the Chemist brand was nationwide.

In the early 1850s John Skelton moved to Edinburgh to set up business. He was successful, but this did not please Dr. Coffin, who went north to persuade him to take a position in the west country.

In the 1850s Wooster Beach paid a visit to England, he and Coffin did not see eye to eye, Beach was educated and an Eclectic, Coffin had stuck to his rather narrow beliefs, and unfortunately like Thomson he became resentful of others who might be more popular than he. Dr. Skelton took on Dr. Coffin's mantle.

A Plea for the Botanic Practice of Medicine by Skelton was published in 1853.

Source on Skelton – the thesis of Alison M. Denham

Dr. William Fox M.D. wrote the very interesting little book, *The Working Man's Model Botanical Guide to Health.* dated 1884. There are twenty pages devoted to Dr. Thomson's Theory and the Life of Dr. Thomson. Thereafter the list of plants as used by Dr. Thomson, the first two cayenne and lobelia, Thomson's hallmark. At that time there were many men like Dr. Skelton and Dr. Fox who wrote books or pamphlets for the majority of people who could not afford to pay for medical treatment. The cures were plants, and as the vast number of folk were living in the industrial areas of England where there would be little in the way of plants they could harvest themselves. It has to be remembered that there were suppliers of herbs by then, Potter, Baldwin and Napier, to name only three. The dried herbs probably came from the Shakers in the USA, or perhaps by then they may have come from Germany and Austria. Certainly by the start of WWI Mrs Grieve notes that the supplies of herbs from that part of the world had ceased.

The Peckham Experiment

Based in Peckham, a district of South London, this scheme initially ran from 1926, then after a break while buildings were improved, started up again to run from 1935–1950.

Participants were invited to take part, at a cost of 1/- a week, about £5 in today's money, that was for the whole family. Some 950 families were invited to take part. It was in essence a scientific experiment to see how people would benefit from what now might be called a 'Nanny State'. There were many positives, health checks, a chance to purchase good organic food to take home, and a canteen for eating in. Exercise in the form of swimming in the specially built pool, physical exercise classes and dancing. It was a cradle to grave approach, advice during pregnancy, then checking on the progress of babies, children, adolescences and the next generation of parents, many meeting at the huge social club. Drs. Williamson and Pearse opened this pioneering scheme.

It has to be remembered that before the NHS came into being in 1947 a trip to the doctor would be 1/- or 2/6 for a home visit. In a way, the whole concept of the Peckham Experiment follows on from the work carried out by the likes of Dr. Coffin, Dr. Skelton, Dr. Fox, and certainly not forgetting Dr. Samuel Thomson who encouraged the less well off a means of looking after themselves and their families.

12.
Apothecaries and Herbalists

The apothecary shop remained a feature for about 150 years after Culpeper's time, to be superseded by the 'chemist shop' This was the place where the doctor's prescription would be made up by the chemist. There were no plants to be seen, only jars with powders and liquids to be made into bottles of medicine, pills, pessaries, ointments and salves.

The chemist would make anything that could be made out of chemicals, matches, fireworks, cosmetics, soaps, disinfectant, and in time they would process photographic film.

Henry Potter

The herbalists hadn't quite gone. In 1812 the young Henry Potter was opening his shop in Farringdon Street, London as 'Seedsman, Herbalist and Dealer in Leeches'. Using his experience of herbs, he made up treatments for all the ailments that his clients needed treating. Now, over 200 years later the Potter's brand is still available.

In 1915 *Potter's Cyclopaedia of Botanical Drugs and Preparations* first appeared, written by R. C. Wren FLS. It gives drawings of the plants with an explanation of their properties. Many plants are indigenous to Britain, and others come from America and the Colonies. The latest edition of the *Cyclopaedia* is a much weightier tome with much more information.

Plants found in the churchyard and the herbal are acorns, bittersweet, black bryony, black nightshade, gout wort, mayweed, ragwort and scarlet pimpernel.

Acorns *Quercus Robur*

The main constituents of acorns are tannins. This is used for its astringent properties. Potter suggests they be powdered down and used as a treatment for diarrhoea.

During wartime roasted acorns were used as a coffee substitute.

Bittersweet *Solanum dulcamara*

Also known as woody nightshade, felonwort

The parts used are the twigs and the bark. The suggested use by Potter is as an anti-rheumatic, and diuretic. It also possesses anti-inflammatory and anti-fungal properties. Not suitable for pregnant women.

Black bryony *Tamus communis*

Potter gives as the medicinal uses rubefacient and diuretic. "The fresh root is scraped and the pulp rubbed into the parts affected by gout and rheumatism."

The stems and berries should not be used, as they will probably cause dermatitis due to the calcium oxalate crystals. There may be some evidence to suggest antiviral properties.

Black nightshade *Solanum nigrum*

Potter suggests that this plant might be used for liver problems. The leaves can be used to poultice burns and wounds.

Gout wort *Aegopdium podagraria*

According to Potter this plant has diuretic and sedative properties.

Mayweed *Anthemis cotula*

Also known as stinking mayweed, dog chamomile

Whilst this plant resembles the chamomile, it should not be used in the same way. It is unpleasant to taste, but according to Potter is antispasmodic, and emmenagogue (used to increase the menstrual flow, and emetic which is used to bring about vomiting).

Ragwort *Senecio jacobsen*

Also known as common ragwort

At one time used as a diaphoretic to induce a sweat, it no longer is suggested for this purpose.

Potter suggests that this plant has been used occasionally as an ointment for rheumatics and other severe pains. Not be taken internally.

Scarlet pimpernel *Anagallis arvensis*

Also known as poor man's weather glass, red chickweed, shepherd's barometer, adder's eyes

Potter says of this plant that it is diuretic, diaphoretic, expectorant. It is a poisonous plant and should only be used by a professional herbalist.

George Baldwin

Some years later in 1844 George Baldwin opened his herbal shop in London. It too has flourished, the shop still sports the traditional wooden furniture and cabinets. Baldwin's sell a great many preparations, and still offers dried herbs.

Their catalogue is full of the many popular British herbs, as well as including others from across the sea.

Duncan Napier (1831-1921)

In Edinburgh when Duncan Napier was opening the door of his herbalist shop, did he have time to read I wonder? If so, he'd have found that the story of Cosette in Victor Hugo's *Les Misérables* was very like his own. Both adopted by a so called 'caring' publican's wife, his treatment was brutal as was that of his fictional counterpart. It was not uncommon for folk to adopt children who would spend their precious childhood in drudgery and be rewarded with beatings, and starvation diet.

Beatings of children with sticks in those far off days seemed perfectly acceptable, thankfully that is not the case today.

On a few occasions Duncan did get the chance to have a spell on an estate in the village of Penicuik, outside Edinburgh. He delighted in the outdoors, being amongst the trees and the plants. The joys quickly disappeared upon returning to Edinburgh. As a teenager he worked unbelievable hours in a baker's shop, bread had to be baked ready for delivery to clients early in the morning. Any time off he devoted his life to plants.

Napier gives an account of his personal history that was eventually found in his papers; he details the sheer misery of his childhood. When still a boy had been told the whereabouts of his birth mother who had abandoned him to his fate. She had a shop, and without revealing who he was, he did patronise her shop to make small purchases just to be around her.

When out on his rounds as a baker's boy he met the kindly Mr John Hope, a man most caring who encouraged Duncan to give up drink (it should be noted that almost the entire population drank beer at that time, as most water proved to be hazardous). He was encouraged to become a Christian. This was a turning point for Duncan. He had observed how drink ruined people's brains, and quickly reduced them to poverty. It was no life at all.

One summer evening Duncan met fellow plant collector, Mr Kaistrey, a Polish gentleman who happened to be the President of the Edinburgh Botanical Society. He invited Napier to join the society, and in no time Napier impressed the membership with his superior knowledge of herbs. He knew what they were used to treat, and where, in and around Edinburgh they could be found.

Still employed as a baker in 1854 he took a wife, a very dear soul who supported all his endeavours. Napier at that stage found some time to devote to learning skills as an herbalist, buying a second hand copy of *Brooke's Herbal*, full of colour plates for plant identification. Later he purchased Dr. Skelton's *Medical Advisor*. This allowed him to be his own family practitioner. There may have been a small chance of Napier hearing about, or reading about Dr. Skelton's time in Edinburgh. John Skelton practiced in the early 1850s before Dr. Coffin turned up to reclaim him as one of his own, thereafter sending Skelton to the West Country.

In time friends and neighbours called on him to help with various medical conditions, so he eventually, started his own business. Napier found premises in Bristo Place. His friend and mentor Mr John Hunt helped financially. It was a risky business, there were already Thomsonians, Beaches and Coffinites operating in Edinburgh. Napier thought it wise to continue with the bakery until he was sure of success. In no time at all it was necessary for him to be engaged totally with the business. People came in great numbers, the shop stayed open late into the evening to accommodate everyone. Herbs had to be gathered from the countryside around Edinburgh, and making use of the train journeys to Fife, to Aberdour and Burntisland allowed for himself and his sons as they grew older to collect the herbs.

Duncan Napier's business flourished, he treated many patients for whom there had been no cure. In 1878 bigger premises were needed. This shop was just a few doors down from the original one. It was furnished in the Victorian fashion, mahogany counters and shelves, gleaming brass and shinning glass cases, and that is how I remember it when I was introduced to it as a student. It was a mysterious, dark place to go into, in an era of dazzling Formica and fluorescent lighting, this was a different kind of experience.

I purchased the inexpensive soaps and shampoos to make my grant go further, also the rose-hip teas. These came in a foil paper, much like a stock cube, to be dissolved in boiling water.

I have a vague recollection of an older bearded man standing at the back of the shop, and believe that he would have been the herbalist ready to offer advice if need be.

There is some information as to the herbs that Duncan Napier collected and from where, but no information on what they were used for.

On a recent visit to Edinburgh I briefly met herbalist Dee Atkinson who has now taken over the Napier's business. Wonderful that it has survived almost 160 years.

13.
English, Scottish and Irish Folk Medicine

England

Lark Rise to Candleford was described by Sir Humphrey Milford, who was head of the Oxford University Press, as the most important book he had published in all the years he had worked there!

The author, Flora Thompson takes us back to the hamlet Juniper Hill in north-east Oxfordshire. For writing purposes she renamed the hamlet as Lark Rise. Her books (originally a trilogy) were based on the diaries that she kept of day to day life in pre-industrial rural England during the 1880s and early 1890s. What makes her work unique is the fact that she actually lived within the hamlet. It was her own personal experiences rather than the work of an academic looking in.

Life for the agricultural labourers was harsh. The rented cottages were basic, without running water, and unsanitary outside privies. The work was relentless and hard, pay hardly enough to keep body and soul together.

It was a hand-to-mouth existence. The keeping of a pig ensured some meat for part of the year, it was air dried above the fire, slices were cut for meals, and the lard used as a butter substitute. Milk was not readily available and more likely to be purchased to fatten up the pig. It was observed that the children were healthy and sturdy, and there were many of them, families of ten were not unusual. They were hardy, and expected to play out of doors in all weathers. They often had runny noses and chilblains, but rarely seriously ill.

Each cottager had a garden to produce vegetables. Berries were gathered from the hedgerows for jam. Parsley, sage, rosemary and thyme were grown for flavourings, and lavender to scent the best clothes. Pennyroyal was probably grown as a contraceptive but, given the size of families, one wonders if it worked. Those who had knowledge of the medicinal herbs were few and far between at this time, the old knowledge was dying out. Of the herbs planted, horehound was used with honey for sore throats and chest colds. Chamomile tea helped ward off colds, and could soothe nerves, and particularly useful after confinements.

Yarrow was gathered from the countryside by the armfuls to make Yarb beer. This would be taken to the fields by the men, and also drunk by the women at home when thirsty.

From the hedgerows, sloes, blackberries and elderberries were made into preserves, what better way to take vitamin C before the oncoming winter.

Cowslips, dandelions and coltsfoot were also used, without specifying what they could be used for.

As to medicinal care in the hamlet, there was none. Doctor's fees were beyond what the labours could afford. Thankfully health was generally very good.

Flora remembers a time when a young curate came to the village. He had been a medical student and he kept a small dispensary in his home. In a charitable fashion he set about helping the community to better health. This resulted in 'illness' being the main topic of conversation in the neighbourhood. Everyone had a need for the pills and potions made available to them. When he eventually left, everyone went back back to normal.

> The general health of the hamlet was excellent. The healthy, open air life and the abundance of coarse but wholesome food must have been largely responsible for that: but lack of imagination may also have played a part. Such people at that time did not look for, or expect illness, and there were not as many patent medicine advertisements then as now to teach them to search for symptoms of minor ailments in themselves.

When it came to the arrival of the newest members of the community, this was undertaken by the midwives within the hamlet. They were knowledgeable and clean older women, whose experience was trusted. The local doctor too had faith in them, and knew that if he was called out it had to be an emergency. This saved him a lengthy drive over poor roads, particularly hazardous at nights.

Eventually district nurses came into being. Flora observed that they were superior to the people in the hamlet and often made them ashamed of their poverty, especially if it was clear that the patient did not process whatever it was that the nurse needed. "The Midwife was a neighbour, poor like herself, who could make do with what there was, or, if not, knew where to send to borrow it... Poverty's no disgrace, but 'tis a great inconvenience" was a positive way of reflecting on the problem.

However poor the people were in the rural areas, it was nothing as compared to those who had to move into the towns and cities.

Whole families forced to live in a single room in a tenement, sleeping on rags or piles of straw on the floor, throwing their waste out into the streets which would be collected at night to fertilise the fields. They had none of the familiar sights and sounds of the country. There were professional herbalists to help, and treat them with sympathy and charity. There were also the 'snake oil' salesmen, who sold 'miraculous' cures with impunity.

Scotland

North of the border there was a belief that the visit of King George IV to Scotland in 1822 had popularised the land of the mountains and the floods, but not so. Before then there had been an interest led by men of science. Thomas Pennant (1726 –1798) from Flintshire, Wales had a great curiosity about the natural world. Like most men of his time he had travelled through Europe, but Scotland was waiting to be discovered by the naturalists.

Together with botanist Rev. John Lightfoot and Rev. J Stewart they travelled through the west of Scotland taking in the islands on that side of the country.

Lightfoot was a Fellow of the Royal Society. As a botanist, he noted the plants used for healing. His book *Flora Scotica* was published 1777 and the illustration on the cover depicted the creeping buttercup, Ranunculus reptans.

A more famous duo braving the unknown regions of Scotland were Dr. Samuel Johnson with his friend James Boswell. This resulted in the travelogue written by Johnson *A Journey to the Western Islands of Scotland* was published in 1775.

By the time of King George's visit, orchestrated by Sir Walter Scott, tartan and kilts became the rage, having been suppressed after the Battle of Culloden in 1745.

On a dull day when I thought I had come to the end of my discoveries, I happened to notice plants growing out of the flint wall on the cold north side of the church, close to the east end. For once it was not ivy, but hart's tongue fern. Also two ferns, one the conventional type, the other a small clump of tiny leaves which I discovered to be wall rue.

The following information is from Tess Darwin's *The Scots Herbal*.

Hart's tongue *Phyllitis scolopendrium*

The Scots Herbal gives the usage as ointment for piles, wounds and scalds.

Ferns

In general, many varieties of ferns were known as the plant to rid the body of worms. In the world we live in now, worms are a rarity. Well, I thought so, but a quick check on-line proves this is not the case. It is not something people like to talk about !

Wall Rue *Ruta muraria*

For such a small herb it seems to have been invaluable in the Scottish Highlands. It was something of a cure-all, and used to help with conditions related to the respiratory system, breathlessness and coughs; skin problems, dandruff, scalp sores, ulcers of the skin; a blood purifier; for kidney stones, ruptured spleens, and rickets. Quite a find !

Puffball *Lycoperdon perlatum*

Puffballs have been found in the Neolithic settlement in Orkney. They may have been used as a wound dressing, the inside of the Puffball is astringent, which will arrest bleeding.

Other than that, the dried remains might have been used as fire-lighting material.

Groundsel *Senecio vulgaris*

Gaelic name *am bualan* (the remedy)

Groundsel was known as a poultice for skin problems, the following was written by Martin Martin author of *A Description of the Western Isles of Scotland*:

> To ripen a tumour or boil they cut female jacobea (this name also seems to apply to Ragwort) small, mix it with some fresh butter on a hot stone, and apply it warm; and this ripens an draws the tumour quickly, and without pain; the same remedy is used for women's breasts that are hard or swelled.

Herb robert *Geranium robertianum*

The name it is known by in Scotland is 'cancer wort'. It was a highly regarded plant and used to treat cancer, as well as wounds and skin diseases. Might it have been a successful cure for cancer? If not, why use the name?

Herb robert is often used in homeopathy and aromatherapy oils.

Dog's mercury *Mercurialis perennis*

This plant was found on the Isle of Skye by Gaelic-speaking doctor, Martin Martin.

It was used to provoke vomiting and diarrhoea. Martin Martin trained in Montpellier, France, and spent a great deal of time gathering herbal information in the Highlands and Islands of Scotland in the 1660s.

Culpeper cautions agains the use of this plant, "there is not a more fatal plant than this."

Ireland

Making the Cure by Dr. Patrick Logan was published in 1972. He looked at folk cures from Ireland, mainly from the regions of Cavan, Leitrim and Longford.

Dr. Logan writes with great respect for the practitioners, those were people who couldn't afford a doctor's fees, and they did what they needed to keep well.

From the author :

> Many of the men and women who practiced it (folk curing) were intelligent and honest and believed in the efficacy of their treatment... I will be happy if people learn that those who practised folk medicine did good for their patients... almost all illnesses – over 80% of them – will get better no matter what treatment is given to them... Even today the best medicine is reassurance, and the ability to reassure a patient does not always go with a medical degree.

There is evidence that plants found in a bog in County Antrim from the Mesolithic and Neolithic period had medicinal properties, according to Harley and Lewis (*Flora and Vegetation of Britain*).

It is amazing to think that our distant ancestors may well have used the plants for much the same conditions as we might do. Also to think that at the time Dr. Logan started his research in the 1940s many of the cures were still being used.

Docks	nettle stings
Ivy	juice to clear chest -corns – skin cancer
Dandelion	leaf sandwich for tuberculosis
	chew, suck and swallow juice to clear chest
Coltsfoot	boiled in milk given to children with asthma – respiratory

Foxglove	protection from fairies – emetic action
Oatmeal	applied to heart area with bandage for nine days
Blackberry	diarrhoea – digestive
Nettles	boiled for worms
Pellitory	gravel – urinary
Self Heal	gravel – urinary
Elder	ringworm – skin
Puffball	stops bleeding
Plantain	macerated, applied to wound
Sorrel	chew then spit onto wound
Yarrow	whitlow poultice
Moss	for wound dressings
Crowfoot	blistering for headaches
Barley	water for gravel – stone – urinary
Charlock	jaundice
Buttercups	jaundice – piles
Ragwort	leg ulcers – wounds
Burdock	blood purifier
Moss	wounds

Dr. Logan's book had a few surprises…

The use of manure from birds and animals.

Besides plants, our forefathers used things that today we would find disgusting. The idea of using 'dung' as a treatment in our well-ordered world of hygienic and pristine hospitals, makes us sick at the mere thought. But should we be living in the past, dung was an ingredient used by the medical profession, just as in Dr. Withering's day…
dung of peacock, pig and horse.

It became a staple of the folk curer. This material could be a very effective plaster. The famous Doctor of Divinity and Naturalist John K'Eogh (1681 – 1754) recommended as a treatment for burns, for hot gout, for hot tumours and bee stings a plaster of cow dung. It was a readily available solution to a burning problem !

K'Eogh recommended sheep's dung for many health problems, but not for whooping cough. Dr. Logan however had heard of a treatment from West Cork, that used sheep's droppings boiled in milk, and given to the patient would cure whooping cough. The fresh dung from a female calf could be applied to Erysipelas (also known as St Anthony's Fire) according to K'Eogh.

Goose dung could be used in milk for jaundice or used with hog's lard to treat ringworm.

Many years ago, I remember talking to a historian about folk cures. She mentioned the goose droppings, and suggested what the goose ate would have affected the cure once it had gone through the digestive process. What would geese like to eat? The obvious item on their diet would be 'goose grass', otherwise known as cleavers. Often 'goose grass' was cooked before being fed to the goslings. Cleavers is indeed known as an herb to help with liver problems, and to prevent or treat jaundice. !!

More recently 'poo' has been in the news, civet coffee, hugely expensive, rated as the best coffee in the world. In the wild the cat like civet eats coffee cherries, and the end product becomes Kopi luwak, not everyone's cup of tea, or coffee.

Similarly Moroccan argan oil is not just sold as oil, but is now used in shampoos and moisturising products. The oil is the end product of the tree climbing goats who eat the fruits of the argan spinosa tree. The journey through the goat's intestines softens the husk, then the Berber women sift through the poo, and grind the seeds to produce the oil.

And finally on this matter, animal and human waste would end up on the midden heap, thereafter used to fertilise the fields to enhance the food crops for the next season as our farmer forefathers had done.

I was particularly excited to read Dr. Logan's book. A random conversation with friend Maire resulted in me borrowing this precious old book. The reason for this excitement, my grandfather's family came from Cavan and settled in Galloway in the south-west of Scotland. His mother and grandmother were herb wives and midwives. It had been a skill learned from one generation of women to the next. I had always hoped that there might have been an old herb book to be discovered, but of course there was no real need when small children became the apprentices to their mothers, and from an early age were soon as knowledgeable as their elders.

Meadowsweet *Spiraea ulmaria*

This is a short account of how this once sacred herb gave its name to the most famous drug in history, aspirin. It is an interesting and convoluted story.

Meadowsweet, a beautiful summer flower has been used by the ancients, to ease pain, bring down fevers and to soothe the stomach. More recent research attributes many more uses for this plant. Its most famous active ingredient is salicylic acid, which it shares with another famous plant, the willow. The following tale looks at salicylic acid in the history of medicine from the times of earliest man, to 1899 when aspirin was launched.

It was the willow that was noted in ancient Egyptian papyrus scrolls. Throughout Roman and Greek periods, the famous physicians Hippocrates, Celsus, Dioscorides, Pliny the Elder, and Galen all used willow in their treatments. Then as fashions go, it ceased to be considered.

The modern story begins with a country parson, the Rev. Edward Stone. In 1763 Rev. Stone wrote a fulsome account of how he discovered the curative properties of the willow bark. He sent this report to the Royal Society, which was then published. Ague (a condition that caused fevers, aches and pains) and malaria were common illnesses then, particularly to those who travelled to India and Africa. Treatment required quina the medical preparation from the cinchona tree, also known as Peruvian bark which was imported, and expensive. The Rev. Stone, while resting under some willow trees happened to taste the bark, noted its bitter taste reminiscent of Peruvian bark, and decided to experiment. Over a period of five years he proved the efficacy of this treatment on those of his parishioners who were suffering malaria or ague type symptoms.

A century later a young scientist at the tender age of twenty-eight was to become a Fellow of the Royal Society for his amazing accidental discovery of the colour purple. William Perkin, when a student of Chemistry, under the tutelage of his German Professor, was asked to synthesise quinine, a substance that had been isolated in 1820. The experiment didn't work, instead he produced a wonderful purple dye. The dyes opened up the way to staining material that could be observed under a microscope, thus of great benefit to the pharmaceutical industry. At present the dyes are being used to aid the search into a vaccine for malaria, which is almost where he started! At Imperial College Hospital the cancerous tumours are stained to help target drugs to the right spot. Sir William Perkin was subsequently named the 'Father of the Chemical Industry'.

As a result of Perkin's findings, dyeing works became big business and flourished in Britain and Germany. At the same time chemists were isolating active ingredients from plant materials, such as nicotine, caffeine and strychnine. In 1828, salicin was isolated from willow bark, but proved to be challenging to synthesise. As it was, doctors did use it on patients, but it damaged the stomach lining. The Bayer factory turned its attention to working on ways to synthesise this potential medicine. Italian scientist Raffaele Piria then went on to discover salicylic acid in 1838.

This preamble seems to have taken us a long way from the beautiful meadowsweet!

In 1830 an apothecary – pharmacist, Johann Pagenstecher used the plant meadowsweet to treat pain of toothache and rheumatism. To save himself time, he made a tincture of the plant, rather than repeatedly gathering it. He reported his experiment to the Swiss Journal. As a result of this article Karl Lowig of Berlin experimented with the tincture, thought he had found a new substance, and named it SPIRSAURE after the meadowsweet.

Later when Raffaele Pirias published his work in 1838, Lowig realised the substance he had discovered was also salicylic acid. The big problem became how to synthesise this useful chemical. There followed sixty years of almost finding the answer; then in the spring of 1899 three scientists working for Bayer, finally produced the elusive pill. Scientists Dresser, Eichengrün and Hofmann finally managed to synthesise the salicylic acid. The three scientists agreed to use the old Latin name for the meadowsweet, spirea, to become ASPIRIN. This drug could bring down fevers, and relieve pain, just as the plant had done. This was the first 'wonder drug' of all time.

It has recently come to light that the man who truly discovered the aspirin was Arthur Edward Eichengrün, a talented scientist with many discoveries to his name. In 1941 he paid a visit to the Hall of Honour in the Deutsche Museum and saw displayed the white crystals of aspirin, acknowledging the success of Hofmann and Dresser, not him! Tragically, being Jewish had precluded him from getting the credit he so rightly deserved.

– References *Aspirin* by Diarmuid Jeffreys. *Mauve* by Simon Garfield (the story of William Perkins).

The Old Days

Herbalist

Back in the 1980s I knew a lady studying to be an herbalist. She said that plants were grown and harvested to the phases of the moon. What a magical idea! Gardeners also knew that plants do well if that rule is observed, and many households purchased Old Moore's Almanac annually. This publication gave information on the planting and harvesting times. It was first published in 1764. Theophilis Moore, a scholar, linguist, mathematician, and nicknamed the Irish Merlin, produced this essential guide for the gardener. His Almanac was the byword for farmers, fishermen and gardeners.

The Almanac came into our home every year. It amazes me to think that my great grandmother might have used the Almanac to guide her in the planting of her herb garden in Cavan, and later in Garliston in Scotland.

14.
Mosses for World War One

Sphagnum moss *Sphagnum cymbifolium, papillose, palustre*

I had been writing monthly articles for the village magazine about the healing plants to be found in the churchyard. It was winter, all the colourful flowers had come and gone. So I didn't expect to find anything worth while. However, the moss on the gravestones caught my eye, they had taken on greater importance without the usual competition. Being wintry, damp and wet, the moss had a new greater significance, being now green and fulsome. In the dry summer months, it was dull and brittle. Coincidentally it was January 2014, somewhere at the back of my mind I knew it had connections to the First World War. Some research followed.

Medicinally it was known as a wound dressing, and, referred to as far back as 1014 in the Gaelic Chronicles. Wounded soldiers used mosses, sphagnum or whatever was to hand on the battlefield to stuff their wounds and staunch the bleeding.

By the time of the Great War it soon became apparent that the need for field dressings could not keep up with the demand. There was insufficient cotton wool, due to the difficulty of bringing it into the country, and what was available was necessary in the production of munitions. Following the example of the Germans, who it is believed 'reinvented' sphagnum moss, sphagnum became a very effective substitute. Cotton wool would only absorb where it made contact with the wound, whereas sphagnum had the ability to redistribute the fluid away from the wound. Sphagnum was better able to deal with the suppurating battle wounds due to its great absorbent capacity, also of great benefit it contained antiseptic properties.

Of course most soldiers in battles sustain serious and severe injuries. What made a great difference in 1914 was that sepsis was a considerable problem. The filthy state of trench warfare caused all manner of infections, the mud entering the wound on the fabric of the uniform carried multiple contaminations.

In Scotland, Edinburgh surgeon Charles Walker Cathcart and Professor Isaac Bailey Balfour, Regius Keeper of the Royal Botanical Gardens, came up with the idea that the wounds could be stuffed with moss. They went on to discover two varieties of sphagnum, papillosum and palustre which proved to be best at staunching blood and could speed up wound healing. They launched the drive to gather the material from peat bogs. This was a very noble endeavour and involved the old and the young. There are stories of Boy Scout troops complete with pipe band going off to gather in the bogs for the day. In Shetland children were given time off school to help the war effort by gathering the moss.

Cathcart's model soon spread to Ireland and to areas in England, such as Dartmoor, where bog moss was abundant. By 1917–1918 collections were being made in Canada, mostly under contract from the British War Office.

Tim Sandles, in his *Legendary Dartmoor* tells of the dedication of folk harvesting the moss, working in knee deep bogs. Some men not able to go to the front felt that they were 'doing their bit' in this way. The gathered sphagnum had to dry outside, as full of moisture, it was exceedingly heavy. When light enough to carry it was taken to a depot, a germ free environment, that was whitewashed and disinfected. Women attired in spotless overalls and caps set about removing any unwanted debris from the sphagnum. Drying was done by laying out over heated pipes. Once dried, the pure moss was measured into two ounce pieces and packed into flat muslin bags which measured ten by fourteen inches. Finally the bags were passed through a solution of corrosive sublimate by a worker wearing rubber gloves, then each bag was mangled to remove the moisture, and dried off. The dressings were made up into packets of a dozen each, wrapped in paper, and prior to being sent abroad were packed into bales of a hundred dressings covered with waterproof sheeting, to keep the whole germ free. A two ounce dressing could absorb up to two pounds of moisture. The nature of the plant allowed the moisture to distribute through the plant cells, therefore the wound of the soldier needed changing less frequently. The Prince of Wales took a keen interest in the work in Dartmoor, providing the depot and the drying equipment.

– Sources *The Kindly Sphagnum Moss: An Unsung Hero?*
Peter Ayres *Legendary Dartmoor* Tim Sandles

I completed this section on 11.11.2018. It seemed appropriate.

Healing plants in time of war

Sadly battles and wars are nothing new, but the weaponry is more dangerous now. History if full of the heroes and the vanquished. In the past it has to be remembered that the foot soldiers were no more than farm labourers who were obliged to fall in behind their Lord and do his bidding.

Unlike professional fighting men, the lads from the hamlets and villages would not have decent protective clothing or finely honed weapons, nor would they have had the services of Florence Nightingale or Mary Seacole.

Soldiers knew that they needed to look to themselves and do their best to heal from their wounds. Jumping through the smoke from St John's wort in the mid summer fire was no guarantee that they might survive. Mosses were useful plant material to help plug a wound. The following plants could be gathered prior to the battle, those might have been:

Hedge woundwort *Stachys sylvatica*

The name suggests its uses as an herb; wound wort for wounds and cuts. It is a styptic, and one can understand that it would have been sought out after a battle. Recent research confirms that the plant can not only staunch bleeding, but has an antiseptic property.

Yarrow *Achillea millefolium*

Also known as soldier's woundwort

The yarrow has antiseptic, astringent and wound-healing qualities. The link to Achilles tells of certain stories that Achilles knew how to use this plant to heal battle wounds.

Shepherd's purse *Capsella bursa-pastoris*

It has traditionally been known as having styptic, haemostatic or astringent qualities, which can arrest bleedings, both internally and externally. This is just one of many plants with this quality, and was sought out as treatment for wounds on battle-fields, certainly during the First World War.

Self heal *Prunella vulgaris*

Also known as brunella

This is a treatment that goes back to the days when brunella (as it was known in Germany) was used by garrisoned soldiers. It has similar qualities to yarrow, in that it can staunch bleeding.

Cinquefoil *Potentilla reptans*

Tannins give cinquefoil its astringency, which makes it a useful plant for washing wounds, and it can staunch bleeding, both internally and externally.

15.
Mrs Grieve's
A Modern Herbal, 1931

Mrs Grieve published her *Herbal* in 1931

My copy of the *Herbal* is in two paperback volumes. They are a great asset for anyone wanting to study herbs. There are hundreds of herbs from the UK, and from the USA and the Colonies featured.

Many of Mrs Grieve's entries hark back to the days of Culpeper and Gerard, and, they in their turn refer to Dioscorides, Galen and Hippocrates. Therefore reading it is like leap-frogging back in time.

Mrs Grieve was born Sophia Emma Magdalene Law, but known as Maud. Her grandfather owned a linen mill, probably in Edinburgh. Her father James, and his brother David moved to London to further the sales of their linen. Born in 1858, Maud was orphaned at the age of eight, it seems that she was split up from her siblings and taken into care by her Uncle David and his wife. Upon the death of her uncle she moved to Edinburgh with her aunt, and there met her future husband, William Somerville Grieve.

There is a gap in her story, Maud would have been about twenty years old when she went to Edinburgh, and about seven years later was in India with her husband. She may well have learned about plants in the Edinburgh Botanical Gardens, and learned to paint at the College of Art.

Her husband's cousin was Symington Grieve a naturalist and archaeologist. He was vice president of the Edinburgh Botanical Society, a Fellow of the Royal Physical Society and a fellow of the Scottish Antiquarian Society.

Maud and her husband settled in Calcutta, William managed the Bally paper mill from 1878 – 1894. By 1906 William and Maud were living in Chalfont St Peter. They named their home The Whins, perhaps a memory of the plant common in Scotland.

Maud created a medicinal herb garden. She gave opportunities to women wishing to work in horticulture. The business was named The Whins Medicinal and Commercial Herb School Farm, Maud tutored the whole process from the planting through the harvesting to the selling.

Mrs Grieve was fifty six years old at the outbreak of the war. She threw herself in to the production of herbs desperately needed to keep the pharmaceutical companies supplied; she also wrote leaflets to educate others.

Mrs Grieve had made a well deserved name for herself, at the British Scientific Products Exhibition in 1918 where she was exhibiting, the following appeared in the catalogue:

> An exhibit which opens up to nurses a vista of an interesting hobby, which may also be a work of national utility, is that arranged by Mrs Grieve, F.R.S.H. who has a School of British Medicinal and Commercial Herb Growing at The Whins, Chalfont St Peter, Bucks, which represents an organised determination to recapture from Germany and Austria the Herb Growing Industry, which those countries have won from Great Britain. Before the war we spent

annually £200,000 on importations of drug-yielding Herbs, which we could have grown. What's more interesting for a nurse living in the country than the cultivation of medicinal herbs? It is further of interest that the demand for properly trained herb growers far exceeds supply, and good posts are obtainable for students when proficient.

Mrs Grieve created a considerable amount of literature, her pamphlets, papers and books are now housed in the Special Collections Division at Edinburgh University.

As a result of all the writing that Mrs Grieve was creating, Mrs Hilda Leyel was drawn to suggesting that a new *Herbal* could be created, largely out of the material that had already been published. Mrs Leyel some twenty-two years younger than Mrs Grieve seemed to breathe new life into the idea of a book of up to date herbal information. Mrs Leyel was a writer herself of a great many books, she was scholarly, and had set up The Society of Herbalists in 1927, and at the same time introducing the high streets to a chain of shops bearing the name 'Culpeper'. More than an herbalist in the old fashioned sense, the shops sold soaps, toiletries and cosmetics as well as attractive herbal preparations to the clients.

Mrs Leyel advised and edited the *Herbal*, and when herbalism came under attack by the Pharmacy and Medicines Bill in the House of Lords in 1941, she and friends managed to soften the proposals, to allow members of the Herbal Society to avail themselves of the treatments offered by the organisation.

The *Herbal* was not a best seller at the time of publication, but almost ninety years later it is regarded as a classic, and like Culpeper's *Herbal* it has stood the test of time.

Plants featured in the *Herbals* of Mrs Grieve.

Slender thistle *Cardus tenuiflorus*
Spear thistle *Cardus lanceolatus, Cirsium vulgare*
Creeping thistle *Cardus arvensis, Cirsium arvense*
Woolly thistle *Cardus eriophorus, Cirsium eriophorum*

Thistles are a very handsome group of plants, but vicious.

As a child I was told that the thistle saved the Scots from the English, In the days when advancing armies had either no foot-wear, or shoes without sufficient protection, it would have been agony to tread on one. The howls from a soldier who stepped on one alerted the Scots. It seems that this story was nearly true, it was the Norse invaders arriving on the Coast of Largs, Scotland, in the mid 1200s, removing their footwear to be truly silent, until a thistle made contact with a bare foot. Consequently the thistle became the Scottish emblem.

The Scottish motto translated from Latin to English read, 'Nobody interferes with me with impunity' or in the Scots tongue 'Wha Daur Meddle Wi' Me'.

In late summer the purple head gives way to lots of downy parachutes by which the plant reproduces its self, very effectively. Children in the early part of the last century busied themselves collecting down from a number of plants, thistles included, to stuff pillows.

The medicinal part of the plants are the roots and leaves. Mrs Grieve states that the ancients had used this plant as a specific in the treatment of cancer, and the juice could be used to treat cancer and ulcers.

Culpeper suggested the juice for cricks in the neck, and good for children suffering from rickets.

Bullace *Prunus domestica*

Mrs Grieve tells us that the bark, root and branches of this plant are 'considerably' styptic. Almost in every way it resembles the blackthorn, but without the thorns, and branches covered in lichens. In the spring I constantly examined the flowers of both, and could find no differences between them. Seemingly in France the bullace is used in the same way as the sloe.

Scabious, field *Knautia arvensis*

Mrs Grieve states that the name scabious suggests a scab, a scaly sore, which comes from scabies, which was a form of leprosy. This pretty plant was thought to remedy this condition. The generic name Knautia from the Saxon doctor, Knaut.

Gerard concurs with Knaut, "The plant gendereth scabs, if the decoction, thereof be drunke certain daies and the juice used in ointments… being drunke, procureth sweat, especially with Treacle, and atenuateth and maketh thin, freeing the heart from any infection or pestilence."

The following two plants are very similar but with their own characteristics.

Purple dead nettle *Lamium purpureum* and **Henbit dead nettle** *Lamium amplexicaule*

The purple dead nettle has heart-shaped leaves with a purplish tinge to it. Mrs Grieve tells us that the reddish flowers have shorter petal tubes than that of the Archangel, (white dead nettle). This is good for the bees with shorter tongues than the bumble bees, therefore attracting another species.

The henbit is a smaller plant. The slender rose-coloured flowers are more pronounced that those of the purple dead nettle.

Both plants have styptic properties.

16.
War Collections

During the First World War it became apparent before the end of 1914 that it was not going to be over by Christmas as had been hoped. As an island nation the country was in danger of running out of food and drugs. Most of our herbs had come from Germany. There had been an attempt made to collect what was available in Britain, engaging members of the public to gather foxgloves, horse chestnuts, rose-hips and much more, but without proper supervision and instruction, much of this was unusable, plants mixed up with others, not dried properly, or not categorised correctly.

The one thing they did manage to do with great success was the harvesting of the moss for the wound dressings.

Just twenty-one years later another World War, and lessons had been learned.

By 1941, The Ministry of Health established a Vegetable Drugs Committee at Kew. This time proper instructions were given as to how to gather, dry, and bundle the herbs. This involved the ladies of the Women's Institute, Boy Scouts and Girl Guides. While many of the plants are safe for collection, there are some that needed careful handling, foxgloves and autumn crocus for example, both potentially poisonous. Children gathered rose-hips and nettles.

Even in recent years countries riven with war in the conflict in Eastern Bosnia 1992 –1995, edible wild food and medicines were gathered.

This is exactly why herbalist Thomas Bartram wrote his *Cyclopaedia*, and Mrs Maud Grieve wrote pamphlets on healing plants, later to become her *Herbal*. Who knows what is round the corner?

At the time that medicinal herbs saved the English home front, penicillin was just emerging as a pharmaceutical drug; But physicians and botanists most likely did not realise that medicinal plants also often have antibiotic properties. In fact, virtually all medicinal and culinary herbs and spices can stop the growth of at least some bacteria. For instance, various mints and tansy (all collected and used medicinally in England during the war) are antibiotic to pathogenic strains including Streptococcus and Staphylococcus. Why? The medicinal secondary compounds of plants often function against bacterial and fungal attack – especially in plant roots, where compounds tend to concentrate. I often wonder that if we continue to overuse antibiotics and antiseptics, we will again need medicinal herbs as pharmaceuticals – this time for their antibiotic properties.

– This article written by Judith Sumner, botanist and author of *American Household Botany: A History of Useful Plants, 1620–1900*.

The following are found in the churchyard:

Black horehound, rose-hips, foxgloves, cleavers, burdock.

Herbalism between the wars, self help

Folk medicine

Gabrielle Hatfield's book *Memory, Wisdom and Healing* tells the story of communities living during the period between the wars, and how they managed with the herbs they had available. This triggered my own recollections and thoughts of treatments during the 1950s.

Much has been written about herbalists, however, this book looks at the oral tradition of ordinary people looking after themselves. The people being interviewed had childhoods in the early part of last century, and, in many cases because of the closeness they had to their grandparents, their reach into the past was considerable, especially if their grandparents in turn talked of memories of their own grandparents. Before the days of television and radio families would gather round the fire on a cold night and talk of the past. Often to the point of constant repetition "Did I ever tell you about…?" In The countryside evenings like those would have been the norm. Repetition was key to the learning. All of this was not a long time ago in the grand scheme of things, considering just how long man has been around. Thanks to the media and social media we can know so much about many trivial things, but are so lacking in many other ways.

The following accounts were recorded by Gabrielle Hatfield:

> The interviewees had worked on the land, and had great experience of the countryside. People in the past could offer a great many solutions to health problems. They were quite healthy, working out of doors, and the occupations would have been very taxing. This period

looked at the years between the wars, but before the inception of the NHS.

Only in an emergency would a family call a doctor. It would cost two shillings and six pence, a considerable amount out of a a farm labourer's wages. A visit to the doctor's surgery, (which would often be be a room in his home) would cost one shilling, which included the medicine.

Each community would manage their own health care, there was usually a man or women who would be known for their skills in times of need. Some would gather herbs and keep the dried plants in brown paper bags, hanging within their homes marked with signs or letters according to what the herb was and how it could be used.

Sometimes the chemist (as they used to be known) could offer medicinal advice and prepare a treatment for the client.

The following plants featured in the book grow in the churchyard:

Gladwyn, ivy, common mallow, musk mallow, elder, hawthorn, plantain major, plantain ribwort, lesser celandine, primrose, honeysuckle, self heal, poppy, lime, St John's wort, cleavers, shepherd's purse, blackberry, cow parsley, foxglove.

17.
Cancer Herbs

Plants found in the churchyard that have been used in the treatment of cancer

There is quite a list of them, not all carry equal weight in terms of what they contribute, many are useful components in the treatment as a whole.

Please note – cancer can only be treated by the medical profession, and anyone offering herbs or advice of a cure could be breaking the law.

Cancer has been around from earliest times, and not just from the time Greek physician Hippocrates gave name to the crab-like growth, cancer.

Recent discoveries of a two-million-year-old foot bone in South Africa point to the evidence that cancer was present in our ancient ancestors.

And it has been with us ever since ! Herbs have been central in the treatment of cancer and up until about four hundred years ago, the only solution.

One of the first written records on cancer cures came from St Hildegard of Bingen. It was for violets. She created a recipe with goat fat, olive oil and the pressed juice of violets. This made a salve that could be applied to the affected area. Today research is been carried out into the benefits and efficacy of the violet.

Hildegard seemed to understand metastases, secondary cancerous growths in other places in the body. For this she advocated yarrow tea to stop its spread. As a visionary she believed that the need to find the cures in plants came from God.

In Medieval times Doctor Odo of Meuse (Lorraine, France) promoted sheep's sorrel as a cure.

There were a number of herbs/plants in the graveyard that were used in supporting rolls as cancer treatments so to speak, agrimony, blackberry, blackthorn, common sorrel, foxglove, mugwort, mullein, St John's wort and yarrow.

They were used in combination with burdock, dandelion, plantain, red clover, sheep's sorrel, violet and yellow dock.

In the early years of the last century there were two notable practitioners of cancer treatment outside the bounds of the medical profession. Texan Harry Hoxsey carried on the family tradition of curing people of cancer. His grandfather had noted a horse with cancer seeking out plants which seemingly made the cancer disappear.

Hoxsey's father and grandfather carried out secret treatments, and in time people suffering from cancer would beat a path to their door for a cure. Harry felt compelled to carry on the practice, and thereafter fell foul of the law. The story is an interesting and very long one, and is the subject of books and documentaries. In the fullness of time Harry took his practice over the border into Mexico along with qualified staff to give the patients the herbal treatments. There are a number of therapists with clinics in Mexico; Dr Max Gerson known for his carrot juice cure for cancer also practices over the border.

In Canada a nurse by the name of Rene Caisse had been given an herbal recipe from an Ojibwa Native American. This proved successful in the treatment of breast cancer. It contained burdock root, sheep's sorrel, slippery elm and turkey rhubarb. It is made into a tea.

This she named 'Essiac', Caisse backwards.

There has been a great deal of controversy surrounding the two treatments.

Jethro Kloss (1862 – 1946). Regarded by some as the American 'Culpeper', in the sense that his book *Back to Eden* has never been out of print. Indeed, the originals are highly sought after, as the modern copies have been modified, and not as written originally.

He dedicated his life to learning, and teaching about nutrition, personal rights, freedoms, and herbalism. Kloss espoused healthy eating and habits, the naturopath approach. He was shocked at the rise in cancer cases. He saw constipation as the main problem, stagnation, the poisoning of the gut. Like other naturopaths Kloss blamed white flour and white sugar, foods all denatured to appeal to the food fashions of the day. He too suggested plants that could rid the body of cancer, red clover, burdock, yellow dock, violet, dandelion, chickweed and agrimony.

Kloss was friends with John Harvey Kellogg, the man famed for introducing the Americans to the simple breakfast of 'Corn flakes', making them from boiled wheat, and rolling them out thinly to produce the flakes. His younger brother William added sugar at a later stage. It was a great deal healthier than the traditional breakfast of meat, biscuits and gravy, washed down with an alcoholic beverage. Many people who were used to the heavy work on the farms, moved into towns and cities, and the huge breakfasts they once needed were unsuited to the new sedentary life style.

Rudolf Breuss (1899 – 1990) an Austrian who maintained that cancer lives on solid foods taken into the body, and that cancerous growths will die if a patient drinks only vegetable juices and tea for forty-two days. It seems that he was able to practice without fear of prosecution, although the medical profession took a very dim view of his treatment methods. In his kidney tea recipe: horsetail, stinging nettle, St John's wort and knot grass.

Breuss also promoted herb robert tea: "Vital for all malignancies, especially if you have received radiation treatment, because the tea contains a small amount of radium."

When I was child there was little mention of cancer, it seemed a shameful thing, and I understand that people would rather attribute a death to tuberculosis than to cancer. There seemed to be very few cases of it then.

When the family had eaten soft fruit of the plum family, the stones were collected and when dried my grandfather cracked them open and he shared the kernels around the whole family. They were very bitter. In recently years whilst studying I have found out about laetrile which comes from the kernels of the apricot family, they are said to have anti-cancer properties, and could be used to treat cancer. However concerns about cyanide poisoning mentioned in the press prevented people from using them.

In 1974 Ernst Krebs gave a lecture at the Second Annual Cancer Convention at the Ambassador Hotel in Los

Angeles, California. He was extolling the virtues of the apricot kernel and its ability to cure cancer. It was known as laetrile, a vitamin, number 17 of the B vitamins. This vitamin is present in peach, nectarine, plums, cherries, apple seeds, and from the churchyard, bullace. Remarkable claims were made for B17, but of course they contain cyanide.

Information on Ernst Krebs – *Cancer: Why we're still dying to know the truth* by Phillip Day

Some years ago, there was a scientist at Newcastle University, Monica Hughes who conducted experiments to see if cyanide could kill cancer cells. Another foodstuff being examined as a cancer cure was tapioca also containing cyanide. Once this disgusting stuff was on the pudding menu fairly frequently !!

18.
Aromatherapy

Egyptians

The perception of aromatherapy is that it is a rather new and fashionable 'spa' treatment, but it has a very long history, thousands of years in fact. The Egyptians were famous for their methods of extracting oils from plants. They distilled them using heated water, pipes and collection bottles. The process would result in the essential oil floating on the top of the water, therefore giving two separate products. In the case of rose petals, this process resulted in rose oil, the most costly of all the oils, and rose water that could be used as perfume or in cosmetics prepared at the same time. Oils were also used in the preparation of embalming the dead before being mummified.

The Egyptians were the first people recorded to be using oils, science has proven this from the mummies found in the tombs. The oil certainly worked, and made a good job of preserving the bodies. They were obviously experts some 5,000 years ago.

Aromatherapy in modern times

René-Maurice Gattefossé – the true founding father of Aromathérapie.

Gattefossé was born in Montchat near Lyon, France in 1881. His family owned a business making perfumes and cosmetics. Gattefossé was both chemist and scholar.

The following is an account of Gattefossé's remarkable discovery of the powers of lavender oil.

> In 1910 French chemist and scholar René-Maurice Gattefossé discovered the virtues of the essential oil of lavender. Gattefossé badly burned his hand during an experiment in a perfumery plant and plunged his hand into the nearest tub of liquid, which just happened to be lavender essential oil. He was later amazed at how quickly his burn healed and with very little scarring.

Wow. This was the story that appeared in many of the books I read at the time of my earliest interests in aromatherapy.

However, according to Robert Tisserand, the actual facts are somewhat different. In Gattefossé's own words in his 1937 book he describes the momentous discovery after he was burned thus:

> The external application of small quantities of essences (Lavender) rapidly stops the spread of gangrenous sores. In my personal experience, after a laboratory explosion covered me with burning substances which I extinguished by rolling on a grassy lawn, both my hands were covered with a rapidly developing gas gangrene. Just one rinse with lavender essence stopped "the gasification of the tissue." This treatment was followed by profuse sweating, and healing began the next day (July 1910).

Tisserand goes on to explain what gas gangrene is, today it would be known as *Clostridium perfringens*.

> Gas gangrene is a potentially fatal infection, and was the cause of many amputations and deaths in the First World War. Although traumatic gas gangrene is

rare today, 25% of those who contract it still die. It is caused by infection of a wound, most commonly by Clostridium perfringens. Onset is rapid and dramatic (though it normally takes 1 – 4 days from the time of infection), with bacterial toxins causing tissue death and subcutaneous swelling and gas. Sweating is one of the early symptoms of infection. Since the bacterium is most commonly found in soil, Gattefossé's rolling in the grass might have precipitated the infection.

This incident in Gattefossé's life was timely. It was four short years away from the total carnage of the fighting in the trenches which was to kill so many young men. Gattefossé perfected certain oils for use as antiseptic, anti-viral and anti-fungal for disinfecting the hospital wards.

Later in life Gattefossé returned to the lavender industry, and gave a great deal of backing to the farmers concerned with the growing and distillation of the lavender to the most useful and recognisable oil that we know today. The 'ladies' from Victorian and Edwardian times used lavender, it was known to dispel headaches. However, lavender does not grow in the churchyard, but it has been a necessary part of the story!

Jean Valnet 1920-1995

Dr. Jean Valnet was born in 1920 in Châlons-sur-Marne France, and died in Vulaines-sur-Seine in 1995. He was an army physician and surgeon, and studied at the Ecole du Service de Sante Militaire et Faculte de Medecine in Lyon, graduating as a doctor of Psychiatry, Microbiology, Colonial Medicine and Surgery in 1945.

During the Second World War he worked for the French Resistance for which he was awarded Légion d'Honneur and the Croix de Guerre (six citations) for his actions.

Dr. Valnet spent time in the Indo-China wars, where, when running out of treatments, turned to cabbage to fight war wounds, very successfully! He may have remembered stories about cabbage being used to treat many injuries at home in France.

In 1948, Valnet chose to prove the value of essential oils in scientific terms, and indeed is regarded as the co-founder along with the chemist Rene Maurice Gattefosse, of modern aromatherapy.

Dr. Valnet continued his research of the plants, and published many books on his findings, *Aromatherapy, Treatment of the Illnesses by the Essences of Plants* (1964), *Dr Nature* (1972) and *Herbal Medicine – Treatment of Illnesses by the Plants* (1972).

He was a corresponding member of the International Centre of Biologic Research in Geneva, giving lectures and sharing his research through essays on essential oils. Valent's forte was anti-infectious properties of actions of essential oils. Knowing all of this, it is frankly puzzling as to how hospitals frequently succumb to outbreaks of all sorts of infections, when essential oils might hold the solution.

I chanced upon a small piece of footage from an interview on line with Dr. Valnet, expounding his theories of the use of phyoto-aromatherapy uses of the oils. He said that 60% of modern medicine was plant-based. The essential oils were particularly useful as an anti-bacterial agent. It was excellent in the treatment of infections, but more effective if used with non-plant agents, iodine, sulphur and magnesium. By including the non-plant material, the effectiveness could be increased to 90%.

Valnet was at pains to explain how dangerous certain oils were, some could induce seizures. The practitioner using the oils in the treatment of others needed to be very careful about the dosage.

Robert Tisserand

Since the 1970s Robert Tisserand's name has been linked to aromatherapy.

At an early age his mother taught him about aromatherapy, and he decided that was exactly what he wanted to do. He effectively brought aromatherapy to England. His first book was written in 1977, *The Art of Aromatherapy*. He set up the Tisserand Institute of Aromatherapy to promote the oils, and train therapists in their use. Robert Tisserand no longer lives in the UK but has settled in the USA to spread the word on the usefulness of the essential oils.

Aromatherapy for Healing the Spirit by Gabriel Mojay

In the introduction Mojay writes, "It is often said that the source of illness has its roots in the depths of the soul. Indeed, it is a belief that was held even by Plato, and in traditional societies by the medicine man."

This is frequent theme in this book, and well recognised by those practicing holistic therapies.

Mojay looks at the plants that have powerful effects on the emotions, and can therefore help with the physical healing needs. Besides the physical uses of the following plants they can each offer spiritual and emotional support thus:

Cedar Wood	strength	endurance	certainty
Marjoram	comfort	contentment	compassion
Yarrow	protecting	mollifying	healing

The above plants are all found in the churchyard.

Having an Aromatherapy Massage

1. For those who like a Spa type of massage or aromatherapy, this is the perfect way to unwind. This combined with the choice of oils can make for a very pleasant experience. One can choose to be 'rejuvenated', 'revitalised', 'balanced', 'soothed' or 'detoxed'. The therapist will have oils ready to use according to your treatment. All the oils will be safe for this purpose. A questionnaire regarding state of health should be filled in beforehand so that there should be no chance of using an oil that might hinder rather than help the client.

2. Visiting an aromatherapist is different. While it is still a pleasurable experience, a client may go to have a particular health issue tackled. Problems experienced might require the use of an oil that is: analgesic, anti-biotic, anti-depressant, anti-inflammatory, anti-septic, anti-spasmodic, anti-viral, expectorant, hepatic, hypotensive, mucolytic, nervine, and so on.

The aromatherapist would make a selection of oils to benefit the client, BUT taking great care to choose an oil that is not contraindicated. Powerful oils come with warnings, for example if the client suffers from epilepsy, is pregnant or breast-feeding, or has sensitive skin; or when treating babies and small children.

As a therapist I marked the tops of my bottles with tiny blue, red, yellow and green stickers just as an extra reminder that I needed to be careful in the use of certain oils.

3. Finally, there are another tier of practitioners, clinical aromatherapists. They work in hospitals, and have a vastly superior knowledge, and a greater understanding of the workings of the human body. In the 1990s the Lewisham Hospital London, trialled the use of marjoram on patients suffering from high blood pressure. It did indeed work at normalising the blood pressure, but frequent massages would have been necessary to stabilise the situation.

Two types of oils

The essential oils are the ones that contain the ingredients to bring about the healing process. They must not be applied to the skin directly. Therefore a few drops of the essential oils must be added to a carrier oil. Popular oils are almond, or grape seed oils. the usual balance is 3% essential oil to the carrier oil.

The carrier oil helps with the massage process, enabling the hands to glide effortlessly over the skin.

The Providers of the Oils

Oils are very much part of the treatment, it is not just about nice smells. In fact there are some oils that do not smell nice at all, it is the active ingredient that is important. In a way it is like using herbs, but instead of being internal, the oils are absorbed through the skin. The skin is the largest organ of the body.

It is worth knowing that not all oils are the same, generally the more expensive they are, the better they are. The quality depends on where they were grown, and how they were processed.

Of the plants found in the churchyard, the following are used as essential oils:

Cedar atlantis

A very complex oil obtained from the wood of the tree. The wood itself was used by the ancients for making chests, the oils warded off the pervading insects from spoiling the fabrics stored. The Egyptians used the oils in embalming, and also for perfumes and cosmetics. Medicinally it is used for urinary tract infections.

Marjoram

The oil can be used to alleviate toothache, can relieve colic, and to bring on menstruation. It also can regulate blood pressure.

Violet

Violet oil is exceedingly expensive, and whilst it has pain relieving properties, it would be unlikely to be used as such. It may be used to improve the quality of the skin. The violet has been used to relieve coughs and catarrh.

Yarrow

Claims to help with skin problems, urinary tract infections and digestive problems.

Bio Carriers

Hazelnut   absorbs easily into the skin

Phytocomplexes

Lime blossom   anti-bacterial, stress reliever
Meadowsweet   anti-bacterial, pain reliever
Rose-hip   eczema, psoriasis, menstrual problems
St John's wort   soothing, emollient, moisturising
Ivy   stimulating and toning
Horsetail   soothing, emollient, moisturising

In the 1990s having studied aromatherapy, I became a Voluntary Therapist in the Community for the local hospice. This involved simple massage, using aromatherapy oils to bring about some small relief. Constipation was a common problem, using suitable oils to massage the stomach worked very well. Massage had to be very gentle, but the touching element was so important, especially to folk for whom touch generally meant some procedure to be undergone. About that time a book on *Therapeutic Touch* by Dorores Krieger came to my attention. It did not promote 'healing' or 'reiki', as hospitals at that time preferred not to promote those ideas, Nurse Krieger encouraged the idea that touch is a very powerful tool to help patients cope with serious illness.

Hospitals have come a long way and now accept that there is a need for treatments like aromatherapy, and indeed the Mayo Clinic offers aromatherapy at a number of its clinics. Writing on the benefits of aromatherapy, Brent A. Bauer M.D. acknowledges that there might be some benefits such as: "Relief from anxiety and depression, improved quality of life, particularly for people with chronic health conditions and improved sleep." It is heartwarming to see aromatherapy being embraced for the well being of the patients/clients. For some time aromatherapy was derided by a company called 'Quackwatch' as Scents for Cents, as an altogether useless therapy.

It is noted that essential oils used in aromatherapy are not regulated by the Food and Drug Administration.

Remembering my friend and fellow student of Aromatherapy, Julie O'Brien who passed away in September 2020

19.
Bach Flower Remedies

The Bach Flower Remedies come under the heading of medicinal plants. The little bottles of drops are inexpensive and can be purchased on the high street, and after being around over eighty years are more popular than ever. Many people use them for feeling down, or depressed, and there is benefit, in that they feel better for the experience.

There is so much more to it than that. Whatever goes on in our minds generally causes an adverse reaction in our bodies. Of course, not everyone who suffers low self-esteem will necessarily share the same kind of illness. It is not that straight forward. The negative emotions will have a knock on effect within our bodies, the condition might just be a cold or headache, but if the state of mind is not addressed, the 'small' illnesses will manifest itself into something more undesirable.

Dr. Bach said that it was necessary to treat the cause rather than the symptoms.

Over 200 years ago René Descartes, philosopher, mathematician, scientist and founding father of modern medicine had discussions, wrote letters and papers questioning the body and the mind. Were they one, or were they separate entities? The church very much believed that anything to do with the mind, mysticism, emotion, feelings and the soul belonged to God and the church, so they were happy for Descartes to dissect bodies to further medical enlightenment, but the mind was off limits !

And so, for many years the mind and body were treated separately. Many doctors may have disagreed. At the turn of the 20th century a number of doctors wishing to understand more about cancer kept notes on the moods of their patients, as they tried to establish a link.

In 1902 Swiss-born psychiatrist Adolf Meyer was director of the New York State Psychiatric Institute. He initiated a system of record keeping known as 'mental hygiene'. Notes were kept on the mental state of patients with a physical illness. This was to ascertain if there might be a link between physical and mental health.

Dr. Edward Bach (1886 – 1936)

Around the time of the First World War a young house surgeon at the University College Hospital London was observing the patients whilst his colleagues were more interested in their conditions. Patients were largely ignored, they were just medical specimens, without names or status. He did something unusual for that time, he engaged with the patients, and noted that when a particular worry was lifted from them, their physical situation improved.

That young doctor was Edward Bach.

Dr. Edward Bach had a method of treating people with 'depression'. He understood just how debilitating this condition is. It holds us back and does not allow us to be the people the we should be. Depression as we know it today is a blanket term for many negative emotions, and the treatment is very much a 'one size fits all', and in a great many cases patients will not be able to live without medication.

> "Healing with the clean, pure, beautiful agents of nature is surely the one method of all which appeals to most of us."

– Dr. Bach

Edward Bach was born in Birmingham in 1886, his greatest wish was to become a doctor. However, he had to work with his father in the family brass foundry. He was a very sensitive person and he observed his fellow workers and the state of their mind. He noted that this related to their physical conditions. Eventually his father supported him to realise his dream, initially he studied medicine in Birmingham, then at the University College Hospital in London. There he became a house surgeon, and also treated private patients from his consulting rooms in Harley Street.

In 1917 at the age of thirty he was working on the wards dealing with the broken souls of the soldiers back from France. One day he collapsed whilst on duty. He suffered a haemorrhage. The cause was a tumour, which his colleagues removed. He was given three months to live.

As a bacteriologist and pathologist Bach had been working on research into vaccines into bowel nosodes. Disregarding the warning that he would not live beyond three months, he got himself back into the laboratory, and with every day that went by his health improved, he was doing something he loved, his life's work. His commitment to achieving this goal seemed to carry him through, and he went on live for another twenty years. His work on the nosodes was promising, and recorded in a number of medical journals. Bach decided to further his vaccines by accepting a new post at the London Homeopathic Hospital, and eventually refined his seven bacterial nosodes. The nosodes were:

Proteus, Dysentery, Morgan, Faecalis alkaligenes, Coli mutable, Gärter and Baccilus No.7. The Morgan nosode for individuals with depression, anxiety and nervousness. The Porteous and Faecalis alkaligenes were irritability, anger, impatience and nervous strain. The Coli mutable changeability and vacillation, and the Bacillus No 7 non alertness and sleepiness. Today these nosodes are used in Europe and America, and are part of the homeopathic pharmacopoeia.

During the period of Bach's life, illness of the mind was occupying a great many medical men. Madness had been known for centuries. The Victorians built great sanatoriums to lock such people away from the public gaze. This may have been kinder than the Bedlam of earlier times

Some years after the church that held Descartes back, they changed their views. It seemed like open season. New treatable mental illness emerged, for the conditions of schizophrenia, hysteria and Alzheimer's disease.

This was a world of Jung; Freud and his *Interpretation of Dreams*; Pavlov and Conditioning, and Otto Rank published *The Trauma of Birth*.

New treatments were being used to treat mental illness, insulin shock therapy, and one that would have likely upset Bach, electroconvulsive therapy. That came in 1938.

Dr Bach was dealing with emotions. Feelings of hurts,

insecurities, fears, lack of confidence, loneliness, a total of thirty-eight conditions that he could alleviate with the plants that he took a number of years to find, each condition having a special plant that would bring relief to the sufferer.

Dr. Bach's preferred method was to treat what was presented by the patient, and the Flower Remedy that suited the condition administered. After a short time when the patient returned, Dr Bach might find another symptom that needed treating. This is called 'peeling the onion'. Thus treating what the patient/client presents with. This would fix the first layer, but it might take several treatments to get to the bottom of the problem. Very often the patient themselves had no idea why they were troubled.

A client might seek treatment because they are down, depressed, not coping and need to be set on the right road again. Unlike a drug for depression, the practitioner can separate all the strands that make up the condition, perhaps fear, troubled by unwanted thoughts, anger, guilt and lacking in confidence.

Dr Bach also truly believed that the physical and emotional states of a person are inextricably linked. He believed that one needed to

"Treat the Cause, Not the Symptoms."

He was a very unusual doctor. While others treated the symptoms, and the evidence of disease, Dr. Bach engaged with the patient; he discovered, and observed the pattern of their illness, how it could improve when a more positive state entered their lives.

Believing that nature had the answer, Dr. Bach began collecting plants, in particular the flowers as the most highly developed part, looking to find something gentler to replace the nosodes.

He gave up his practice in Harley Street,

He set off to Cromer in Norfolk and Wales to allow himself to be drawn to what-ever plant was needed for perfecting a cure for the condition that he himself was experiencing at the time.

Dr. Bach finally settled in Mount Vernon, Sotwell, Wallingford, and with friends Nora Weeks and Victor Bullen set about making the flower remedies from the collected plants, many he introduced to the garden.

Dr. Bach enjoyed woodwork and made much of his own furniture. He lived very humbly, and was very at home in the country, a far cry from the Harley Street Days. Bach enjoyed being with the others in the village, perhaps watching a football match, or enjoying a beer in the pub.

Over a period of time Dr. Bach perfected all the thirty-eight remedies he felt were needed to comprehensively treat all manner of negative emotions.

Bach wanted the world to know that there were solutions to problems that affected people's health and well-being, he gave lectures to that effect.

The medical council were troubled by the idea of one of their own proclaiming that individuals could cure themselves. That was always Bach's idea: Man should be able to heal him/herself.

Before he could be struck off, he resigned his position.

Just after his fiftieth birthday, twenty years after being told he only had three months to live, Dr. Edward Bach died peacefully in his sleep.

One of Dr. Bach's more radical ideas was that we should not need hospitals in the future. That didn't seem feasible to me when studying, but I now understand what he meant. Most disease can be linked to emotional states, whether those suffering recognise it or not. How often as bystanders can we observe the stress and unhappiness of a family member or friend, followed by illness which we knew would be coming. It is said:

"The spectator sees more of the game."

I believe that is true.

At the end of Bach's life he wrote a number of letters to the Medical Council: here are two of them.

To my Colleagues of the Medical Profession

After very many years of research, I have found that certain Herbs have the most wonderful healing properties; and that with the aid of these, a large number of cases which by orthodox treatment we could only palpitate, are now curable.

Moreover, on-coming disease can be treated and prevented at that stage when people say, 'It is not bad enough to send for a doctor'.

But when we gain the confidence of those around that disease should be tackled in its very earliest stages, and moreover, when we are able to explain to them that in the most obstinate and chronic cases it is worth while persevering with treatment, our work will be widely extended. Because we shall have that army of people come to us, days, weeks or months before they otherwise would to have their health adjusted; and secondly, the chronic cases will not only send for us, when they wish for relief of pain or discomfort, but will send to us to continue with their cases in the hopes of a cure being obtained.

The Herbs mentioned can be used in conjunction with any orthodox treatment, or added to any prescription, and will hasten and assist the treatment in all types of cases, acute or chronic, to be more successful.

It is a time amongst us when orthodox medicine it not fully coping with a proportion of disease in this country; and it is a time to regain the confidence of the people, and justify our noble Calling.

The Herbs are simple to every student of human nature to understand, and one of their properties in that they help us to prevent the onset of organic disease when the patient is in that functional state which in either acute or chronic ailments so often precedes them.

Well springs
Sotwell
Wallingford
BERKS
January 8 1936

To the President of the General Medical Council
Dear Sir,

Having received the notification of the Council concerning working with unqualified assistants, it is only honourable to inform you that I am working with several and shall continue to do so.

As I have previously informed the Council, I consider it the duty and privilege of any physician to teach the sick and others how to heal themselves. I leave it entirely to your discretion as to the course you take.

Having proved that the Herbs of the field are so simple to use and so wonderfully effective in their healing power, I deserted Orthodox medicine.

The Following are the 38 plants discovered by Dr. Bach

Agrimony – mental torture behind a cheerful face
Aspen – fear of unknown things
Beech – intolerance
Centaury – the inability to say 'no'
Cerato – lack of trust in one's own decisions
Cherry plum – fear of the mind giving way
Chestnut bud – failure to learn from mistakes
Chicory – selfish, possessive love
Clematis – dreaming of the future without working in the present
Crab apple – the cleansing remedy, also for self-hatred
Elm – overwhelmed by responsibility
Gentian – discouragement after a setback
Gorse – hopelessness and despair
Heather – self-centredness and self-concern
Holly – hatred, envy and jealousy
Honeysuckle – living in the past
Hornbeam – tiredness at the thought of doing something
Impatiens – impatience
Larch – lack of confidence
Mimulus – fear of known things
Mustard – deep gloom for no reason
Oak – the plodder who keeps going past the point of exhaustion
Olive – exhaustion following mental or physical effort
Pine – guilt
Red Chestnut – over-concern for the welfare of loved ones
Rock Rose – terror and fright

Rock Water – self-denial, rigidity and self-repression
Scleranthus – inability to choose between alternatives
Star of Bethlehem – shock
Sweet Chestnut – extreme mental anguish, when everything has been tried and there is no light left
Vervain – over-enthusiasm
Vine – dominance and inflexibility
Walnut – protection from change and unwanted influences
Water violet – quiet self-reliance leading to isolation
White Chestnut – unwanted thoughts and mental arguments
Wild Oat – uncertainty over one's direction in life
Wild Rose – drifting, resignation, apathy
Willow – self-pity and resentment

I was fortunate enough to do my practitioner studies at Sotwell; and lucky to find a good Bed & Breakfast over the fields about a mile away. Wonderful to start and end the day walking around the hedgerows to the little class room behind the house that Bach called home.

There are 9 Bach Flower Plants in the churchyard

Agrimony

This I found to the wild grassy area at the south east of the churchyard.

The words of Dr. Bach as he describes the type of person who relates to this plant:

> The jovial, cheerful, humorous people who love peace

and are distressed by argument or quarrel, to avoid which they will agree to give up much. Though generally they have troubles and are tormented and restless and worried in mind or in body, they hide their cares behind their humour and jesting and are considered very good friends to know. They often take alcohol or drugs in excess, to stimulate themselves and help themselves bear their trials with cheerfulness.

Dr. Bach placed agrimony in Category 5 – for those over sensitive to influences and ideas.

Potentised in and around Cromer, Norfolk 1930

Elm

The elm is part of the hedgerow to the right of the church gate. One can only assume that in the 1950s a grand elm would have stood there. As I've noticed in other places nearby, evidence to this is what is left in the hedge.

Those who are doing good work are following the calling of their life and who hope to do something of importance, and this often for the benefit of humanity. At times there may be periods of depression when they feel that the task they have undertaken is too difficult, and not within the power of a human being.

Dr. Bach placed elm in Category 6 – for despondency or despair.

Potentised in Sotwell 1935

Holly

As one would expect there are a few hollies in the churchyard.

> For those who are sometimes attacked by thoughts of
> such kind as jealousy, envy, revenge, suspicion. For the
> different forms of vexation. Within themselves they may
> suffer much, often when there is no real cause for their
> unhappiness.

Dr. Bach placed Holly in Category 5 – for those over-
sensitive to influence and ideas.

Potentised in Sotwell 1935.

Honeysuckle

The honeysuckle is unmissable, it stands by the gateway to
the church.

> Those who live much in the past, perhaps a time of great
> happiness, or memories of a lost friend, or ambitions
> which have not come true. They do not expect further
> happiness such as they have had.

Dr. Bach placed this honeysuckle in Category 3 – for those
with insufficient interest in present circumstances.

Mustard

When I didn't expect any other discoveries, charlock
appeared within a glorious tangled mat of plants, all of
them competing for space in the old graves. I didn't realise
that this was Mustard until I noticed the Latin name in the

plant book, *Sinapis arvensis*

> Those who are liable to times of gloom, or even despair, as though a cold dark cloud overshadowed them and hid the light and the joy of life. It may not be possible to give any reason or explanation for such attacks. Under these conditions it is almost impossible to appear happy or cheerful.

Dr. Bach placed mustard in Category 3 – for those with insufficient interest in present circumstances.

The mustard plant grows prolifically on disturbed ground and is frequently seen where road works have existed. Sometimes it is confused with rape which turns large portions of the countryside yellow during the farming season, but although the flower-heads are very similar, the leaves and general size of the plants differ.

Dr. Bach first potentised this remedy in Sotwell 1935.

Oak

The oak with the ash trees are situated to the far east of the church, by the spring.

> For those who are struggling and fighting strongly to get well, or in connection with the affairs of their daily life. They will go on trying one thing after another, though their case may seem hopeless. They will fight on. They are discontented with themselves if illness interferes with their duties or helping others. They are brave people, fighting against great difficulties, without loss of hope or effort.

Dr. Bach placed oak in Category 6 – for despondency or despair.

The oak tree is a symbol of the English countryside and depicts the very same nature of the type of person the remedy is meant for – solid, reliable and a pillar of strength.

Dr. Bach first potentised this remedy near Cromer, Norfolk in 1933.

Star of Bethlehem

The Star of Bethlehem and oat were discovered on a May evening in glorious sunshine to the south west of the church in amongst the old graves.

> For those in great distress under conditions which for time produce great unhappiness. The shock of serious news, the loss of someone dear, the fright following an accident, and such like. For those who for a time refuse to be consoled, this remedy brings comfort.

This remedy is one of the five ingredients contained in Rescue Remedy, and its purpose is to relieve the sudden alarm and trauma associated with emergency situations.

Dr. Bach placed Star of Bethlehem in Category 6 – for despondency or despair.

Star of Bethlehem was one of the first plants Dr. Bach found to replace the bacterial nosodes, but he first potentised this remedy as part of his system of Flower Healing in Sotwell.

Wild oat

This was found near the Star of Bethlehem amongst the old graves

> Those who have ambitions to do something of prominence in life, who wish to have much experience, and to enjoy all that which is possible for them, to take life to the full. Their difficulty is to determine what occupation to follow; as although their ambitions are strong, they have no calling which happens to them above all others. This may cause delay and dissatisfaction.

Dr. Bach placed wild oat in Category 2 – for those who suffer uncertainty.

Potentised in Sotwell during 1934.

Wild rose

This forms part of the hedge to the east.

> Those who without apparently sufficient reason become resigned to all that happens, and just glide through life, take it as it is, without any effort to improve things and find some joy. They have surrendered to the struggle of life without complaint. For the type of person who enjoys life and is content the way it is. The remedy would be needed if such a person felt that life was passing them by or felt apathetic, resigned to all that happens. The positive quality of this remedy is greater motivation and enthusiasm for life.

Dr. Bach placed Wild Rose in Category 3 – for those with

insufficient interest in present circumstances.

The one that got away!

Cherry plum

In the spring I discovered the hedgerow alive with the white flowers of the blackthorn and cherry plum, or so I thought. The white flowers were incredibly similar, one on a hedge with huge thorns, the other on a weathered and gnarled small tree, the branch covered in orange lichens. On the last Sunday in July I noticed the fruits were forming, both were round, one bluish/black, the other seemed to be of a dark greenish hue. Also the leaf of the latter plant was pointed, whilst the others rounded and without a doubt blackthorn or sloe. Upon showing it to a lady who knew the churchyard well, she said this 'cherry' was actually a 'bullace'. I understand it makes very good jam.

As the Bible says… "By their fruits ye shalt know them"…

Serendipity

Just at this moment in time I have observed in the media that there are studies going on, particularly with young people, linking the problems in the gut to emotional issues. Information coming out certainly backs this theory. Or, could it be the other way round?

Dr. Bach believed it is the negative emotions that cause the body to be sick.

Simple evidence of the mind registering on the body

embarrassment	red face
sudden shock	ashen face
pre-performance nerves	dry mouth and butterflies in the tummy.

In April 2020 my friend Anne Catchpole passed away. It was she who introduced me to the Bach Flowers, thus inspiring me to study and become a Bach Flower practitioner.

Molecules of Emotion by Candace B Pert, Ph.D

If Dr. Bach had been around in the late 1970s he would have been amazed that science was beginning to understand that there was a link between the emotions and illness.

And probably even more amazed that the scientist was a woman! Neuroscientist Candace Pert was famous for the discovery of the opiate receptor.

Dr. Pert wrote about her experiences working as a scientist in John Hopkins Baltimore. In her book *Molecules of Emotion* she describes in detail the cut throat race to the top when it came to scientific discoveries. Positive results would secure funding for further research projects. She was one of a small team, but strongly asserted that it was her contribution that actually made the breakthrough necessary to get the team past the finishing post so to speak. It was such a significant piece of research that would help pain killers to be specifically targeted to the receptor in the brain to make the drug work. Science in 1970s was very much a male dominated pursuit, and whilst she was part of the team, she would not be honoured in the same way as her male colleagues. Instead of accepting her humiliation quietly as Rosalind Franklin had done (allowing Watson and Crick to be lauded for what Franklin believed was her research) Pert complained bitterly, and the result was that the Nobel Prize was not awarded to any of them in the team. Franklin died of cancer. Pert was beginning to understand the link between the emotions and physical illness. At this point in her life she was comparing herself to Rosalind Franklin and how she had an untimely death. Franklin had not kicked up a fuss, but accepted that that was the game of science, the boys got the top prizes, that was how it was. Pert empathised with Franklin, understanding how the feelings of anger, hurt, resentment, low self-esteem and rejection could, or might have been the link to her ill health and untimely death. Rosalind was thirty-seven years old. Pert continued for many years in mainstream medical research, but then understood that those negative emotions do contribute to ill health.

She then moved into the world of alternative health, giving her findings in the *Molecules of Emotion: Why you feel the way you feel*. Pert died at the age of sixty-seven. She was highly respected by Deepak Chopra who shared the same beliefs.

Louise L. Hay wrote, *Heal Your Body: The mental causes for Physical illness and the metaphysical way to overcome them*. She argues that the mental thought patterns that cause the most disease in the body are 'Criticism, Anger, Resentment and Guilt'.

Long held Criticism will often lead to conditions like arthritis.

Anger turns to conditions that boil and burn and infect the body.

Resentment over a period of time will eat away at the self, perhaps leading to tumours and cancer.

Guilt always seeks punishment and will cause painful conditions.

As a footnote to this section it is wonderful to see that Rosalind Franklin has not been forgotten, there have been a great many posthumous markers to her scientific achievements. In 2019, the European Space Agency (ESA) named their ExoMars rover Rosalind Franklin.

20.
A German, an Englishman and a Frenchman

During the 20th century there were three notable herbalists, and they all lived to the ripe old age of 96. All have left their mark.

They all valued and loved plants and appreciated how they can be used to heal the body and the mind.

Professor Rudolf Fritz Weiss, M.D
Weiss's Herbal Medicine Classic Edition
1895 – 1991

Over many years of studying and reading articles about herbs, the name 'Rudolf Weiss' frequently came up in the references. I finally got a copy of *Weiss's Herbal Medicine Classic Edition*, and discovered he was much more than an herbalist !

Weiss was born in 1895. In 1922 he qualified as a doctor in Berlin, studying botany as well as medicine. More especially Weiss promoted phytotherapy, a science-based evaluation of the effectiveness of herbs testing the empirical values attributed to them. He became known as the founding father of modern German phytotherapy.

During the war his teaching of herbal medicine was put on hold while he served as an army doctor. A spell of seven years captivity followed in a Russian prisoner of war camp.

Weiss retired in 1961. His next challenge was to campaign for the acceptance of Herbal Medicine. Later in 1978 he became a member of the German Commission E which researched 300 plants as to the efficacy and benefits of the popular herbs. The team was made up of scientists, toxicologists, physicians and pharmacists. Weiss was founder and editor of the *Zeitschrift fuer Phytotherapie*, and lectured on current advances in the subject at the University of Tübingen. Weiss's classic book *Herbal Medicine* appeals to both medical doctors and herbalists alike.

The following plants are all featured in Weiss's *Herbal Medicine*.

Grass *Agropyron repens*

Weiss promoted it to alleviate the problems of prostatic adenoma, today known as benign prostatic hyperplasia.

Pineapple mayweed *Matricaria discoidea*

Writing in his *Herbal*, Weiss refers to the findings of French phytotherapist Leclerc that soldiers responded well to pineapple mayweed when suffering from threadworms. Simple infusions were very effective, and not too unpleasant to take.

Silverweed *Potentilla anserina*

Weiss believed that the silverweed would cause diarrhoea to cease, however, when put to the test in the Russian prisoner of war camp, Weiss found that it had limited success, and was glad when the conventional medicine became available.

Had he been allowed to wander from the camp, he might have found the vastly superior…

Tormentil *Potentilla erecta*

Weiss would have used the powdered rhizomes to combat the outbreak of diarrhoea.

One never knows when such a situation might arise, and knowledge of herbs could prove invaluable.

Maurice Mességué
Of Men and Plants
(today known as Of People and Plants)
1921 – 2017

Mességué's autobiography *Of Men and Plants* is one of the most inspirational books I have ever read. This man by the end of his life had earned the respect of many in the medical profession. Although unsought, he acquired celebrity status, treating both the poor, and the rich and famous. He also made a name for himself in the media.

Mességué was born 1921. He writes lyrically about his early years, with passion about his beloved mother, and more particularly, Camille, his father. Camille's family had lived for generations in Gavarret in the Gers region of France. The family lived off the soil, they harvested their food from the wild, both the plants and the animals. They practiced herbalism, and had a reputation for helping their neighbours. Maurice's earliest lesson on the subject came in the form of a 'lime-blossom bath.'

When he was about four years old Maurice remembers a spell of disrupted and fractious sleeping patterns. This would be put right by the special bath. Maurice's mother filled the copper cauldron with hot water. Camille tenderly described the copper as being "Finer than gold, it was like that because it had been a mirror to the sun and the fire."

Mother then added the special golden liquid that was prepared from the lime blossom. Maurice remembered feeling more relaxed and drowsy and the day ended in a perfect sleep. Life continued along those idyllic lines, Maurice expected that he too would be a healer and herbalist.

Camille had learned his craft from his mother. A 'Herb Bible' had been passed down the family. which amounted to a few pieces of paper with poorly written instructions, and drawings of the plants. In the main the teaching had been passed down verbally and demonstrated on the many neighbours who turned to Camille for treatment. There was one visitor to the Mességué's household who called under cover of darkness, the local doctor. His problem was described as 'fluid retention'. Maurice watched in astonishment as the doctor stripped and sat in a hot bath to which nettle, mint, celandine, sage and beard of corn were added. "He was stripped of his clothes, but not his dignity or his monocle."

Camille showed Maurice all manner of things in the countryside. Father and son would lie in the grass and watch the weasel rolling in the plantain (a plant known as an antidote for the bits of vipers) before attacking a snake They watched the mother swallow wiping the closed eyes of her chicks with greater celandine to open them.

This blissfully happy life ended when his father suffered a fatal accident when out hunting. Camille accidentally shot himself whist leaping a ditch. Mother and son found themselves very poor indeed; his mother went into service, and he into a boarding school as a scholarship boy. Through the miserable years he harboured the dream that one day he might practice like his father, or even become a doctor, but alas being poor put paid to that ambition.

Mességué was determined to follow his dreams, healing with herbs he regarded as his birth right. He knew that without the formal training he could not practice. He could not administer herbs medicinally, but chose as his father had done to make up 'macerations' of a few herbs to treat clients in the manner of 'foot and hand baths'. As he was not giving medication to be ingested, he hoped to ensure he would not fall foul of the law.

Maurice did not forget what he had learned from his father Camille, and all the years when behind the walls of the boarding school, he continued when the opportunity arose, to seek out the plants he so loved. One or two of the masters remembered his father and came to him quietly when they had a need of help. Prior to this Maurice had observed the tell-tale signs of a brewing illness, and had in his mind what he would suggest if asked.

The making of the 'macerations'. All Maurice required were his chosen herbs, a bowl and clean water. After chopping the plants, they were left to steep, then strained, the resulting herbal matter left was known as 'marc' and was squeezed out, then discarded. The liquid was bottled for future use.

This liquid would be added to warm water, and the patient would be required to immerse either hands or feet for a period of time. It does sound rather an odd treatment, but herbal actions are absorbed through the soles of the feet and the palms of the hands. It is a practice going back to Roman times.

The war came along, and Maurice found himself working at the postal service censoring letters. He found it difficult to read private mail. In time he took notice of the emotional forces at work; when writers felt down or depressed in one letter, it often followed that the writer at a later date had succumbed to a physical condition. Good news brought about a better state of health. It was when working on the mail that he was plucked out to treat his first paying client. Unbeknown to him this man turned out to be a very important man indeed !

Maurice was asked about his interest in herbal medicine as someone needed his help for a generalised arthritic shoulder. The man needing treatment was a senior official who had suffered his problem for three years and no doctor had been able to help him. Maurice armed himself with cabbage, water cress, nettle, beaten egg white and a small glass of the rheumatic maceration to make a poultice. The maceration contained great burdock, heath, wild camomile, greater celandine, couch grass, broom, lavender and onion. Maurice concentrated on preparing his herbs just as he had seen his father doing. After applying a poultice, he left a bottle of the maceration to be used in twice daily in hand baths. The poor man who had suffered so long was willing to try anything. Maurice saw his patient on two other occasions, he was improving and happy with the treatment. His patient was in fact Admiral Darlan, one of the most powerful people in France at that time. Maurice was devastated when Darlan was assassinated in December 1942.

Mességué then wished to try out his treatments, and finding a vagabond in the streets of Nice with a very bad case of eczema, set about treating him. Supplying the man with bottles of wine by way of payment, he could observe the improvement of his skin condition. In due course, the man's skin did improve.

Mességué like his father was unqualified in the medicinal sense, and had they prescribed herbal preparations to be taken internally, they would have fallen foul of the law and could have been prosecuted and jailed for fraud. He frequently did get arrested for healing. He was never jailed, and had a great deal of support from clients whose health he had turned around. None of his clients suffered any ill effects or indeed death.

In 1968 he had his final court hearing in Grasse. It would be a landmark case for him and all those practicing unorthodox medicine. There were 220 testimonials from doctors and 20,000 moving testimonials from patients. Mességué was not prosecuted. In later years he did appear on television programmes with the lawyer of the Medical Council to discuss matters of health.

During Mességué's long life he had met and treated many well known people, politicians, statesmen, royalty and celebrities. Chancellor Adenauer of Germany and Prime Minister Winston Churchill of England accepted advice from Mességué.

As well as treating the rich and famous, he still had time to treat the poor as his father had done.

His reputation spread throughout France, doctors sent their patients to him when modern medicine failed. Mességué could only describe himself as a healer and herbalist. His treatment method was unconventional, his treatment, using the appropriate herbs for the condition, but only on the hands and feet!

I have chosen one treatment from his book, using the plants familiar to the churchyard.

Shingles
Buttercup – flowers and leaves – one handful
Poppy – flowers and crushed capsules – one handful
Meadowsweet – one handful
Lime-blossom – one handful

Local compress
Foot-and-hand baths

Mességué recommends a lime blossom bath in the case of an overall eruption: 500 grams to a litre of water. Its soothing action can be increased by a handful of poppy, and made milder by two handfuls of mallow (flowers or root) and three handfuls of starch.

Buttercup – known to raise blisters
Poppy – narcotic
Meadowsweet – astringent, pain relief
Lime – hysteria palpitations
Mallow –eases inflammation

n.b. Whilst studying Folk Medicine in Scotland it seems that occasionally treatments were given by putting the plant material into the armpit or groin of a patient.

Thomas Bartram
***Bartram's Encyclopaedia of Herbal Medicine* (1995)**
1913 – 2009

Herbalist Thomas Bartram was an exceedingly knowledgeable and gifted man. He healed his patients by using the plants he loved. After a hospital career he became a consulting medical herbalist in private practice, and served as a council member of the National Institute of Medical Herbalists and also the Society of Herbalists. His home was in Bournemouth in the south of England.

At the age of sixty-seven he embarked upon his epic *Encyclopaedia of Herbal Medicine*. In his book preface Bartram states the following:

> Is it not amazing, after 200 years denigration and ridicule, that herbalism is stronger than ever? At a time of unprecedented demand for natural medicines there would appear to be a need for a comprehensive A to Z compendium of diseases and their treatment. Today, clinical effects of natural medicines are convincingly demonstrated. These were the remedies used by Pythagorus, Galen and Hippocrates. Their use today has been built upon the experience of centuries. Their data has often been confirmed at the cost of human lives – a point often overlooked by research workers. Their use extensively around the world, especially in the underdeveloped countries, exceeds that of conventional medicine.

Having lived through the Second World War, Bartram would have experienced the blockades that hampered supplies of drugs to the United Kingdom. Aspirin manufactured by the Bayer Company in Germany was one such loss. This eventually appeared in a slightly different form from New Zealand as 'Aspro', and this product was available well into the 1950s.

Drug shortage then was a real problem, and necessitated the government to instigate the collection of the much needed, but sometimes forgotten herbs to provided the sick of the nation with their appropriate medicine.

So, first hand, Bartram would know exactly the kind of disruption that could jeopardise lives.

Thomas Bartram worked many years to compile his *Encyclopaedia of Herbal Medicine*. It had been his life's work, and he felt it necessary to create a hand-book detailing medical conditions and suggesting the curative herbs needed for good health. He is therefore preparing his readers for a world that might have to look back to the old trusted and tried remedies of our forefathers, and we should take heed.

After fifteen years working on the *Encyclopaedia*, at the age of 82, Thomas Bartram completed his work. Twenty-five years later this book is much sought after, and is a very good reference book.

Of course, those using the book would have to know what the plants actually look like. Urbanisation is taking over huge swathes of countryside, and flowers are no longer mentioned in the up to date dictionaries. Children are no longer close to nature, and while the *Encyclopaedia* is a wonderful thing, unless the next generation know what they are looking for all might be lost.

In his remedies Bartram most often made up synergistic blends, thus benefiting from more than one treatment, perhaps pain relief in conjunction with water retention for instance. Here are a few examples to those used singly.

Avens – ulcerated colitis, diarrhoea, diverticulitis or Crohn's disease.

Woodruff – migraine, congested liver and to support a weak stomach.

White bryony – rheumatism worse from movement, rheumatic fever, acute – arthritis

Ragwort – for poultice or ointment as treatment for rheumatoid arthritis, – lumbago, gout, sciatica

Rosebay willow herb – weak stomach, gastroenteritis, diarrhoea in children, colitis

21.
Cae Mabon

My personal experience

In the spring of 2007, I chanced upon a flier for a Druid Herb Camp set in Wales. The illustration was particularly beautiful, a Celtic herbalist at work, and through the open window a rainbow descending on the Glastonbury Tor which was mirrored in the lake.

The course was being run by Herbalist Melanie Cardwell MHNH, with contributions from Dr. Angela Paine and Chief Druid Philip Carr-Gomm.

Arriving at Cae Mabon, I found it an enchanted space and place. The land was undulating with the river roaring by. Quaint little buildings and roundels offered students accommodation. There was a grand thatched round house in the Celtic tradition. I found myself sharing a roundel with a turf roof with three other ladies. It was May, and quite chilly, the wind did enter around the doorway and windows. Needless to say, no mod cons. The toilet was a walk away, up the hill, it was what is known as a long drop toilet. Sawdust was chucked down after the business had been conducted. The wash-basin was filled from a fresh rainwater tank. Periodically the deposits from the loos were taken to fertilise the planting areas, just as had been from time immemorial. Ablutions on the first morning, shock horror, a cold outside shower. We did it only once, the ladies and myself had a pact that none of us would bother showering for the remainder of the stay!!! There was a rather ingenious hot-tub sited by the edge of the fast-flowing river. Made mainly of wood, it was filled daily with fresh river water, and heated by a log stove. That was bliss, it reached the required temperature just as dusk fell.

The main purpose of being there was to learn about herbs first hand. Melanie had prepared the course to take in the main functions of the body, heart, kidneys, liver, lungs and skin. We were lectured on how to look after ourselves using the correct food to keep the body healthy. All meals were vegetarian, and healthy living was key. Exercise, fresh air and good sleep were all important.

Plants were the major part of the course. Plants that could help alleviate medical conditions. These were made into ointments, salves, tinctures and oils.

All participants fell into the rhythm of each day, the meals were wholesome, tasty, and free of the things that are not beneficial to good health. There was no alcohol, meat, sweets or chocolate.

Dr. Angel Paine gave a talk on Celtic herbs and their uses. She had just written a book on the subject. There were evenings in the huge round house, evenings of singing, storytelling and poetry. The fire was smoky and sore on the eyes, we were all rather kippered, but the experience was immensely enjoyable.

On a wonderfully sunny day we climbed to the birth-place of Merlin, this involved fording streams, climbing stiles and stone walls, lots of walking, punctuated by stops to hear the Bard, Eric Maddern, telling stories of the life Merlin.

Eventually atop of this magical place all fell silent, each of us with our own thoughts. I remember taking in the rugged little trees, gnarled and twisted, boughs laden with lichens, very much like an illustration from a book of fairy stories.

Not every day was like that, it did rain of course, but the glory came afterwards, walking under the dripping trees with the shafts of sunlight catching the mounds of moss on ancient stones and tree stumps.

Melanie was launching her Herbcraft Course, which I signed up to. There were many aspects to this, but it was essential to get know the dozen or so plants that would be most useful to us, especially if they could be found near to our homes.

Some of the most understated plants turned out to be the most useful. I had hoped to be a 'Sister Cadfael' and be able to find the most interesting and unusual plants ready to supply a small infirmary. This course needed to be more practical, it was sensible to find plants growing to hand. The benefits of doing this was to know what plants were readily available, and where exactly to find them. It was wise to find plants that would arrest bleeding, halt diarrhoea, relieve pain, aid sleep; treat problems of the skin, respiration, circulation, and much more. Many of the simple plants had within them a number of different uses. Living in the country as I did then I made my choices. dandelion, plantain, dock, hawthorn, dog rose, elder, ash, couch grass, nettle.

Once chosen, the studying began. I made many mistakes, school-girl errors! It was all about finding out for myself. I chose to start this study in January, at the beginning of the calendar year. With hindsight, how ridiculous, it is not how nature works. Nature works on unseen until it is ready to reveal itself in the spring. It is a great continuation from one season to the next. There is nothing to see in January, February, and sometimes March even. Trying to distinguish the elder, hawthorn and dog rose in the hedgerow before the leaves showed was tricky. I began to panic as I could find no evidence of dandelions and travelled further from home to try to find them. I was just looking at the wrong time !

The file information on plants recorded thus:

common name
botanical name
plant family/genus species
parts used
collection season/s of the parts used
cultivation and propagation

Observation of the plant was essential. Over the period of the year development could be recorded with photographs, sketches, paintings, leaf pressing, seed collection, in other words getting to know the plant very well.

During the year collecting the parts that would be made into tinctures, teas, salves, ointments, poultices.

> "The life for natures so excellent in its gifts that... it better benefit a man to know one herb in the meadow, but to know it thoroughly, than to see the whole meadow without knowing what grows on it."
>
> – Paracelsus

22.
The Churchyard That Keeps On Giving: The Real Deal

I have amassed a tremendous number of photographs of plants in the churchyard, and very often only discover others when uploaded onto the computer. Sometimes when a plant is spotted that I hadn't seen at the time, I pop back to find it.

On a few occasions I have come across some fungi, and just snapped them. Not something I know anything about, so there was never an intention to write about them. One day as I sat browsing through the images, a voice beside me said, "Oh hello, what have you got there?" I was then reliably informed that they were psilocybin commonly known as magic mushrooms. Almost immediately books were ordered for me so I would have a better understanding of them. Such things had passed me by ! My first encounter was *How to Change Your Mind* by Michael Pollan.

So why the excitement? These mushrooms are being scientifically investigated as a means of helping people cope with post traumatic stress disorder, childhood traumas, depression and anxiety.

It is strangely fitting that as the book nears its end this chapter should, like the first chapter feature the shaman. They were probably the first people to use hallucinogenic plants. They used them spiritually, magically and other worldly, and certainly not recreationally.

Some years ago, a find in a Bolivian cave strongly suggested that a pouch dating from AD 900 to 1170 would have belonged to a shaman. This pouch was made out of three fox snouts, and thought to contain hallucinogenic substances.

Many years ago, mushrooms were thought to be very poisonous, and in certain countries they were not found on the dinner plate. This notion might have come about as they were only thought to be used by the magic man, the shaman.

Psilocybin also known as magic mushroom has now been scientifically proven to help the brain deal with the emotions that cause harm, depression, anxiety, low self-esteem, childhood traumas, and post traumatic stress disorder. Work is being carried out at the Centre of Psychiatry at the Hammersmith Campus, Imperial College in London. Psychopharmacologist David Nutt has been working alongside Neuroscientist Robin Carhart-Harris since 2009 to identify the path of the psychedelic experience. The procedure involves giving the patient a dose of psilocybin then charting the progress by tracking the brain by using functional magnetic resonance imaging and magnetoencephalography (neuroimaging technique for mapping brain activity).

The third member of this group is Amanda Fielding, who has established the Beckley Foundation, and institution to study the defects of psychoactive substances on the brain.

LSD is believed by Fielding to enhance the cognitive function.

David Nutt had been Chairman of the government's Advisory Council on the Misuse of Drugs, unfortunately he used two phrases, "Alcohol is more dangerous than cannabis" and "Using ecstasy is safer than riding a horse." It is possible that he was right, but it cost him his job. Interestingly enough cannabis is at this time being considered as a possible treatment for epilepsy.

There are some serious studies being conducted in the USA at New York University and John Hopkins Psychedelic Research. In carefully controlled procedures, terminally ill cancer patients are being given the chance to try psilocybin to help them overcome their fear, and the stress of dealing with the end of their lives. This is an expensive treatment, involving the patient being cared for whilst on a 'trip'. It can take hours, and has to be done under the proper supervision. What has been truly amazing is that individuals seem to be able to forget their egos, and allow the experience of pure love to overwhelm them.

The person who first suggested this type of therapy was Aldous Huxley. He had hoped that the process of dying could be a more spiritual experience than it otherwise was, and in 1963 at his own end his wife administered an injection of LSD. Huxley had quite an interest in psychedelics, and he featured them in his novel *Brave New World* (1932). In his book he called the drug 'Soma'.

Almost on a daily basis there are reports in the media of people who are treating themselves with psilocybin, micro-dosing, just a little amount to improve their concentration and awareness, to relieve depression and anxiety. Of course, anything to do with magic mushrooms is illegal, here in the UK and in the USA a jail sentence could follow.

At this moment in time the media and internet are awash with accounts of the research that is going on, and also the business opportunities for the investors.

Very recently, certain States in the US have voted to decriminalise hallucinogenic mushrooms. It is only a matter of time before other states and countries follow suit. In the 1960s, at the time of 'Peace and Love', there certainly seemed to be fewer vicious attacks and criminality.

– Source: Michael Pollan *How to Change Your Mind*.

23.
Lichens

Then there are lichens! How could I have overlooked the lichens? They were adorning the flints, the gravestones and some of the trees.

In the spring I became fixated with the hedgerow. The short, trees with gnarled branches were covered in lichens. What I found attractive about it was there were two different lichens growing on the bark, one a bright orange yellow, the other a whitish, greyish green.

My photographs on the computer gave me a chance to fully appreciate the growths. They were quite beautiful.,

The name lichen comes from the Greek meaning 'leprous', referencing lichens as a treatment for skin conditions.

Lichens are an ancient plant species of simple cell construction. They are found growing on stones and tree bark. They behave in a similar way to mosses, they thrive in moisture; survive in drought, only to be revived when the rain falls again.

The more I looked, the more beautiful I thought they were.

It is said that lichens survived when the Earth was hit by an asteroid sixty-six million years ago. It wiped the dinosaurs out, and many of the other life forms too.

Plant material including lichens have been used in the

dyeing of fabrics. By using salt, alum and copper many beautiful colours were produced on linen, wool and silk. The ancient, process was very time consuming.

Dame Diana Mossop includes lichens as part of her Phytobiophysics. This treatment uses the vibrational essences of the plants. Here is how they were used in the preparations:

Orange lichen: skin lesions/candidiasis of the genitourinary tract.

White Lichen: skin disorders, melanoma, skin cancer, virus.

There are many more lichens growing on the gravestones, and on the church walls. This opens up a whole new world of discovery...

24.
Very Up to Date Herbals

I am fortunate to have an extensive range of books dealing with herbs, but there is always room for something new and special. The very 'up to date books' can appeal to everyone, not just the student of herbs.

As one would expect, they give the common name of the plant, the Latin name, the active ingredients, and the plant as used in the past. More importantly they now give the results of scientific research to support the claims made for them.

They are well laid out and beautifully illustrated, especially when it comes to the business of identifying the plants correctly.

Here is a selection from my book shelves.

Julie Bruton-Seal & Matthew Seal, *Wayside Medicine, Hedgerow Medicine*

James Wong, *Grow Your Own Drugs: A Year with James Wong*

Jekka McVicar, *Jekka's Complete Herb Book*

Vicky Chowan & Kim Walker, *The Handmade Apothecary*

All of these beautiful books give recipes for teas, tinctures, ointments, salves, cordials and much more. These can be used to treat the gamut of day-to-day problems for respiratory conditions, skin problems, urinary infections, aches and pains. Also, tonics to be used as preventatives to ward off seasonal ailments.

So just as Elizabeth Winstanley of Quenden did in the 1600s, it is possible to gather and make up many lotions and potions to ensure that the family can have sound good health, even in today's world.

25.
Herbal Medicines

Not so many years ago the advances being made in medicine and the innovations of the pharmaceutical industry made it seem inevitable that the use of herbal remedies in developed countries would decline to insignificance. It is somewhat of a paradox therefore, at a time when there is such an unprecedented number of therapeutic drugs available for the treatment of all forms of disease, that herbal remedies continue to be demanded by the general public. In fact, this demand has steadily increased over the past decade and as a result of enquiries from practising pharmacists, the Royal Pharmaceutical Society of Great Britain commissioned this volume in order to provide factual information on medicinal herbs.

> – Carol A. Newall, Linda A. Anderson, J. David
> Phillipson, *Herbal Medicine* 1996

This book is a guide for health care professionals.

Herbalists who study 'phytotherapy' (a science-based study of plants to evaluate the effectiveness of the herbs), perfectly understand the research conducted listing the active ingredients within each plant. Each plant in the book gives the 'constituents' for example the flavonoids, triterpenes, volatile oils, tannins, glycosides, mucilage and others.

The research for the book was carried out mainly on animals and humans. Contraindications were listed, usually concerning pregnancy and lactation. A qualified herbalist would take everything into account before preparing an herbal remedy, often making use of a number of herbs together.

There are other ways the plants might be tested, for instance, clinical research, laboratory research, international acceptance, safety and the history of the plant. By and large the research carried out for *Herbal Medicines* suggests that the same constituents are used for similar if not the same conditions as might be used in conventional medicine.

Many plants included in the book appear in the churchyard:

Agrimony, avens, burdock, cleavers, coltsfoot, couch grass, cowslip, dandelion, elder, ground ivy, hawthorn, horehound black, meadowsweet, nettle, pilewort (lesser celandine), plantain, red clover, shepherd's purse, St John's wort, wild lettuce, yarrow, yellow dock.

Old plant treatments for today's illnesses, seen in a new light

Bluebell *Endymion non-scriptus*

It has been observed that there are compounds within the bluebell likened to that of water-soluble alkaloids that are being tested in America and Australia. These are thought to be of use in medicine for HIV and cancer. Dr. Alison Watson of the Institute of Grassland and Environmental Research, Aberystwyth, Wales, has been studying the bluebell. She has stated that the compounds might be difficult to produce synthetically, so the bluebell would have to be grown and developed into a medicine. "It is conceivable that one day farmer's fields may be covered in blue carpets of the flowers grown for their commercial value." (Quote from BBC Sci/Tech published January 15th 1998)

Snowdrop *Galanthus nivalis*

During the years of the Cold War, Russia had been cut off from the rest of Europe, therefore Western medicine was unavailable. During that period there were many outbreaks of polio, a devastating illness, many losing their lives or being disabled. In America the iron lung was invented. This helped those suffering to be able to breathe; they were a common sight in hospitals during the 1950s. Many owed their lives to this invention.

Beyond the 'iron curtain' the Russian victims of polio had no such assistance, and they had to resort to their own folk medicine. It was observed that Bulgarian peasants rubbed bulbs and leaves of the snowdrop onto the foreheads of patients.

The treatment appeared to have a beneficial effect on certain neurological conditions. Apparently, the paralysis did not develop after the use of the snowdrop bulb.

In 1951 two Russians pharmacologists, Mashkovsky and Kruglikova-Lvovastarted, isolated the ingredient galantamine from the snowdrop. By 1958 the first industrial process of galantamine had begun in Bulgaria by Professor Dimitar Paskov. This helped alleviate the symptoms of Alzheimer's disease. Galantamine in Eastern Europe had been used to treat neuritis and neuralgia, myasthenia gravis, (chronic muscle weakness), myopathy and post-polio paralysis.

Bringing the story up to date, in the 1980s after the fall of the Berlin Wall, Professor Trevor Walker made an exciting discovery. When working in Eastern Europe he came across Bulgarians growing snowdrops for the galantamine that they would yield. Not something that he thought too much about until a friend developed Alzheimer's. He recalled the time he had witnessed the snowdrop being grown for this purpose.

Galantamine is the recognised ingredient in the successful treatment of Alzheimer's, but it costly to produce synthetically, therefore the solution seemed to be to grow a crop that could supply the galantamine naturally.

And the snowdrop is not the only plant to produce galantamine…

Daffodils and dementia

Daffodils do too!

In recent years Welsh sheep farmer Kevin Stephens turned to farming daffodils when his friend Professor Trevor Walker realised that Alzheimer's could be treated by extracting galantamine from daffodil bulbs. Now they are grown in vast fields at the high altitude of the Black Mountains in Wales. This stressful climate helps the plant to produce a greater amount of galantamine. The drug industry pays £600 per ton of daffodil bulbs, and ten tons are needed to make one kilogram of galantamine. More sheep framers are taking up the daffodil challenge, and it is good for the Welsh economy.

There is a hope that the daffodils will slow the development of Alzheimer's disease… and hopefully keep patients living in their own homes for as long as possible.

26.
Plants are still the thing!

Many years ago while on holiday in Malaysia I went on a group walk with Naturalist Irshad Mobarak. He was lecturing on the medicinal value of the plants found growing close by. It was astonishing to see just what the plants could offer for general illnesses. A pharmacy on the doorstep !

One leaf picked had the power to stop bleeding of a wound, not only that, the leaf also contained an antiseptic, so that germs would not flourish. How Amazing. Surely we could not find the like at home? Well, yes we could. In Britain we have Hedge Woundwort, This plant as it says is a 'woundwort'. It too has styptic and antiseptic qualities. Soldiers of old would definitely have known this plant !

Knowing of my interest in plants, Irshad introduced my husband and I to Dr. Abdul Ghani Hussain, Medical Practitioner and Principal Consultant, Researcher in Traditional Malay & Islamic Medicine. We were graciously entertained to tea, whilst learning about the many medicinal and cosmetic properties of the plants. He did however caution that, in certain circumstances one needed to know when it would be prudent to accept today's conventional medicine. The Malaysian forests have many research scientists searching for the answers for todays ills.

Until recently in the UK we had naturalist and herbalist Jan de Vries. From his base in Troon, Scotland, he travelled around around the country and the world treating patients with his herbal treatments. His story is an interesting one, during his childhood years he experienced the misery and privations of the war in Holland, the land of his birth.

Jan de Vries qualified as a pharmacist, before meeting Dr. Alfred Vogel who persuaded him into the world of herbalism. I was very fortunate to meet him when he was lecturing. He worked tirelessly meeting people, and he also took time to respond to letters, I have one to treasure.

Where we are today.

For many years herbal products were sold in Health Food Shops. Then in the early years of 2000 the European Union deemed it necessary to evaluate those products before granting the right to sell them to the public. Across the board suppliers of herbal preparations had to submit to regulatory standards of the European Union if they wished to continue their business.

Some years ago my friend Dr. Roger Vogel, ophthalmologist and physicist in drug research gave me his opinion on this matter.

He said more than 50% of drugs were in fact based on the active components a plant, there was no doubt about their effectiveness. The question was how the herbal products had been prepared. Who knew how they had been grown and harvested, and the conditions they might have been packaged in? They might have been made up in a garden shed, with dubious hygienic standards.

Under EU rules the herbs could only be marketed if the preparation was made in a sterile laboratory, accurate dosages, properly packaged and labeled. The herbal companies who survived this process were the ones who could afford to present their herbs to the EU to legitimise them.

In 2011 many companies had their herbal preparations approved, but they could not make any claims for the efficacy of the treatment. For the Bioforce brand this meant that the bottle of Hawthorn tincture, for centuries accepted by herbalists for the treatment of heart problems, could not mention the fact on the bottle. A more acceptable way of putting it thus:

'Food Supplements should not be used as a substitute for a varied and balanced diet and a healthy lifestyle.'

Ingredients: Tincture of fresh Crataegus oxyacantha (Hawthorn) berries, extracted in alcohol (50%v/v), together with directions for dosage.

Any further information would be supplied on the promotional literature within the shop, or on line. In the independent Health Food Shops the staff are suitably qualified to help customers, but of course would always suggest that the client should consult their doctor if the problem was of a serious nature.

In the re-vamp process Jan de Vries of BioForce was inspired to have coloured illustrations of the plant on the labels. This showed the plant contained in the bottle. He later changed the name from Bioforce to A. Vogel as a homage to Alfred Vogel the founder of the company. Vogel had the plants grown in the high mountains in Switzerland and Austria, the crop was grown far from any polluting substances, and within hours of harvesting, the plants were being transformed into the tinctures.

With regards safety, herbs like conventional medicine gives recommended dosages, and they must be adhered to.

Few of us saw this coming !

The Coronavirus Pandemic, Covid 19.

All manner of dis-ease have been about since the time of earliest man. In his book *Blood and Guts*, Professor Roy Porter describes in a dozen pages the history of sickness from syphilis, typhus, cholera, smallpox the Spanish Flu and ebola. In 1969 the US Surgeon General stated that the book on infectious disease was now closed !

Two years later President Richard Nixon declared 'War on Cancer', at that time cancer was the second largest killer in America .

Fifteen years after the Surgeon General's pronouncement, HIV arrived.

This latest pandemic has been a very strange time to live through. As yet a vaccine has to be found to bring Coronavirus under control.

Nature has come to the fore in an unexpected way. Recently it has been recognised that spending time surrounded by plants is very beneficial to good health.

The Japanese appear to have been the first in modern days to suggest that taking time out to be with nature, surrounded by nature, to smell, touch, taste, listen to, and see nature has so many health benefits. It was recently suggested that it should be offered on the NHS, but that is not likely to happen. **Shinrin-yoka** or Forest Bathing, was introduced in the 1980s, and now is accepted in many countries around the world. Whilst one can do this for oneself, many people like to be part of an organised group, with a leader taking the party into the forest to allow for the gentle healing to take place.

While the NHS might not have the funds for Forest Bathing, many inner cities doctors do recommend patients caring for plants, and then joining groups to further this interest and share the experience with others.

During the recent lock down, (quarantine) many have discovered the joys of connecting with plant life. From window boxes to gardens, growing became a passion. The recommended daily exercise brought enjoyment and sense of well being, that will probably be remembered as a positive to be taken out of the whole unfortunate experience of the pandemic. Clearer, quieter skies brought the wonder of bird song, and the nightly experience of the starry heavens. For all its misery the year of 2020 might have a lasting impact, and greater understanding that Mother Nature heals.

Sources of information

Over a period of twenty years I had many files of articles from magazines and newspapers, they gave a great deal of information that I found helpful, and have been used as source material. They didn't survive a house move, therefore I am unable to reference them here.

Part One

Ross Alison *Wildlife Sanctuary in a Village Churchyard*

Lewis Stempel John *The Running Hare*

Buczacki Stefan *Earth to Earth*

White Rev. Gilbert *The Natural History of Selbourne*

Wohlleben Peter *The Hidden Life of Trees*

Part Two

1. Beginning of time

Paine Angela *The Healing Power of Plants*

Hopman Ellen Evert *A Druid's Herbal*

Lavender S & Franklin A *Herbcraft*

2. Medieval Fact and Fiction

Chappell Cherry *Grandma's Remedies*

Kourennoff/St George *Russian Folk Medicine*

Rob Talbot & Robin Whiteman *Brother Cadfael's Herb Garden*

3. Tudor and Stuart Times

Genders Roy *The Cottage Garden & the Old Fashioned Flowers*

Gerard John *Gerard's Herbal, The Generall Historie of Plantes*

Bruton-Seal Julie & Seal Matthew *The Herbalist's Bible*

Potterton, Shellard, Stringer *Culpeper's Colour Herbal*

Woolley Benjamin *The Herbalist*

Alison Barnes *William Winstanley – The Man Who Saved Christmas*

Wood Matthew *William Coles*

4. The Smoking Herbs

5. John Wesley and his Primitive Physick. Erasmus Darwin

Wesley John *Primitive Physick*

6. Foxgloves and Dr. William Withering

Uglow Jenny *The Lunarmen*

7. Homeopathy: Less is More

Wells Rebecca *Homeopathy*

Ruddock E.H. *The Lady's Manual of Homeopathic Treatment*

Rose Dr.Barry *The Family Health Guide to Homeopathy*

8. Sweat Lodges

9. The Shakers and their contribution to herbalism

Miller Amy Bess *Shaker Medicinal Herbs*

10. The First Americans

Josephy Alvan M. *500 Nations*

Densmore Frances *How Indians use wild plants for Food, Medicine & Crafts*

11. Thomsonians – Back and forward across the pond & The Peckham Experiment

Eastoe Jane *Victorian Pharmacy*

Griggs Barbara *Green Pharmacy*

Fox William *The Working Man's Model Family Botanic Guide*

Atkinson Tom *Napiers History of Herbal Healing, Ancient & Modern*

Ray John *Essex Naturalist*

Denham Alison M *Skelton Thesis*

12. Apothecaries and Herbalists

Williamson Elizabeth M. *Potter's Herbal Cyclopaedia*

Wren R.C. *Potter's Cyclopaedia of Botanical Drugs & Preparations*

Atkinson Tom *Napiers History of Herbal Healing, Ancient & Modern*

13. English, Scottish and Irish Folk Medicine – Meadowsweet

Thompson Flora *Lark Rise to Candleford*

Darwin Tess *The Scots Herbal*

Beith Mary *Healing Threads*

Barker Anne *Scottish Traditional Plan Lore*

Logan Dr. Patrick *Making the Cure*

Garfield Simon *Mauve*

Jeffreys Diarmuid *Aspirin*

14. Mosses for World War One

Field Studies Council *Guide to Mosses & Liverworts*

Sandles Tim *Legendary Dartmoor*

15. Mrs. Grieve's Herbal

Grieve Maud *A Modern Herbal 1 & 2*
Chappell Cherry *Grandma's Remedies*

16. War Collections

Hatfield Gabrielle *Memory, Wisdom and Healing*

17. Cancer Herbs

Ausubel Kenny *When Healing Becomes a Crime*
Moss Ralph W. *Herbs Against Cancer*

Snow Sheila & Klein Mali *Essiac Essentials*

Day Phillip *Cancer – Why we're still dying to Know the Truth*

Ransom Steven *Great News on cancer in the 21st century*

Breuss Rudolf *The Breuss Cancer Cure*

18. Aromatherapy

Davis Patricia *Aromatherapy an A-Z*

Tisserand Maggie *Aromatherapy for Women*

Worwood Valerie Ann *The Fragrant Pharmacy*

Mojay Gabriel *Aromatherapy for Healing the Spirit*

19. Bach Flower Remedies – Molecules of Emotion

Bach Edward *Heal Thyself*

Howard Judy & Ramsell John *The Original Writings of Edward Bach*

Howard Judy *The Story of Mount Vernon – Home of the Bach Flower Remedies*

Ball Stefan *Bach Flower Remedies for Men*

Howard Judy *The Bach FlowerRemedies Step by Step*

Weeks Nora *The Medical Discoveries of Edward Bach Physician*

Scheffer Mechthild *Bach Flower Therapy*

Chancellor Philip M *Bach Flower Remedies*

Pert Candace B. *Molecules of Emotion*

20. German, an Englishman and a Frenchman

Weiss Rudolf Fritz *Weiss's Herbal Medicine*

Bartrum Thomas *Bartram's Encyclopeadia of Herbal Medicine*

Mességué Maurice *Of Men and Plants*

21. Cae Mabon

22. The Churchyard that keeps on giving

Jackson Brian A. *Mushroom Medicine*

Pollan Michael *How to Change Your Mind*

23. Lichens

Field Studies Council *Guide to Common Churchyard Lichens*

24. Very Up to Date Herbals

Julie Bruton-Seal & Matthew Seal *Wayside Medicine, Hedgerow Medicine*

James Wong, *Grow Your Own Drugs: A Year with James Wong*

Jekka McVicar, *Jekka's Complete Herb Book*

Vicky Chowan & Kim Walker, *The Handmade Apothecary*

25. Herbal Medicines

Newall Carole A, Anderson A, Phillipson David *Herbal Medicine*

26. Plants are still the thing

Prof. Roy Porter *Blood and Guts*

de Vries Jan *Traditional Home Remedies*

Vogel Dr. Alfred *The Nature Doctor*

Bibliography

Wild Flowers	Simon Harrap
Wild Flowers of the British Isles	Ian Garrard & David Streeter
Scottish Wild Flowers	Michael Scott
Illustrated Wild Flowers	Stephen Blackmore
Concise British Flora in Colour	W. Keeble Martin
Wild Flowers of Britain & Northern Europe	Blamey, Fitter & Fitter
Wild Flowers of Britain	Reader's Digest
Wild Flowers of Britain & Europe	Margot & Roland Spohn
Shetland's Wild Flowers	David Malcolm
Flora of Foula	Sheila Gear
Key to Common Ferns	Field Studies Council
Guide to Fruits & Seed Dispersal	Field Studies Council
Guide to Plant Galls in Britain	Field Studies Council
Guide to Grassland Plants	Field Studies Council
The Fungi Name Trail	Field Studies Council
Tree Wisdom	Jacqueline Memory Paterson

Tree Medicine	Peter Conway
Illustrated Book of Trees	B.E. Nicholson & A.R. Clapham
Healing Herbs	William Thomson & Elizabeth Smith
Wild Herbs book 1	Richard Mabey
Natural History of Selborne	Rev. Gilbert White
The Englishman's Flora	Geoffrey Grigson
Weeds	Mea Allan
Herb & Spice Companion	Marcus A. Webb & Richard Craze
The Apothecary's Garden	Anne McIntyre
Complete Floral Healer	Anne McIntyre
New Holistic Herbal	David Hoffmann
The Magic of Herbs	David Conway
Home Remedies & Herbal Cures	Carol Bishop
The Healing Garden	Gay Search
Nature's Medicines	Richard Lucas
History of the English Herb Garden	Kay N. Sanecki
Health from God's Garden	Maria Treban
The Green Pharmacy	James A. Duke Ph.D.
The Healing Garden	Sue Minter
Plants of the Devil	Corinne Boyer

Acknowledgements

To Norman for his love, understanding and support. He has seen me through many projects, but the book seems to have been never ending ! I greatly appreciate his patience and tolerance. My thanks to him with love.

My grateful thanks to all my friends in the church

To Carole Crosby for her beautiful artwork of the plants in the churchyard.

To those who gifted me books:
Effie, Norman, Don & Jen, Colin & Arianne, Jamie, Katherine & Ella Riddell, Amelia & Duncan Murdoch, Georgina White, Jim & Mary White, Will Vogel, Janet & Dick Lanaghan, Iain & Lillias Macduff, Sam, Ian, Roni & Cait Hyslop, Pam Shillito, Mary Millbank, Graham Howell, Gill McCraith, Billie Fraser, Lynsey Hart, Marie Rhodes, Tracey Hicks, Susan Castle, Carole Bowes, Liz Hedge, Pauline Moss, Rebecca Ousley, Helen Carson, Edward Taub, Margaret Jerman.

Fellow therapists whom I have learned from, and shared ideas with :
Margaret Mehta, Anne Catchpole, Caroline Kooy, Julie O'Brien, Hannah Shine, Sarah Gregg, Melanie Cardwell, Ron & Jenny Sambridge, Sonya Hunn.

To those who have inspired me and encouraged me to write:
Jessie Haliburton Burke (Countess of Mayo), Margaret Swain, Sally Howard Smith, Phyllis Cole, Frank Watt, Darren Linton, David Bowes, Peter Sanders, David Morson.

Friends who helped identify the plants:
Audrey Rodgers, Iris Wood, Roger Darlington.

Technology
Without the computer there would be no book,
Jamie gave me my first lap top and encouraged me to write
about herbs.
Luke Downing has taught me how to use the computer,
Peter Podgorski has used his expertise in sorting out the format.

This has been a long project and during the period of ten years
I have met many wonderful people who have given me new
thoughts, different ways of seeing things, words of kindness and
support.

Grateful thanks to all.

> *"Many people died while the herbs that could*
> *have saved them grow on their graves"*

– Father Sebastian Kneipp
Bavarian Priest 1821-97

9 781913 962685